CHILDREN OF ALCOHOLICS

A Bibliography and Resource Guide
Third Edition

by

Robert J. Ackerman, Ph.D.
Indiana University of Pennsylvania

Health Communications, Inc.
Deerfield Beach, Florida

Robert J. Ackerman, Ph.D.
Indiana University of Pennsylvania
Indiana, Pennsylvania

Library of Congress Cataloging-in-Publication Data
Filed

© 1987   Health Communications, Inc.
         Enterprise Center
         3201 S.W. 15th Street
         Deerfield Beach, FL 33442

ISBN 0-932194-48-6

Cover design by Reta Kaufman

FOREWORD

This bibliography and resource guide is designed to provide valuable information for those interested in helping children of alcoholics of all ages. Additionally, it can be used as a "bibliotherapy" tool for children of alcoholics themselves who want to know more about the disease of alcoholism and the impact that it may have on their lives. Isolation and silence can be replaced by awareness and knowledge.

Although not an exhaustive list, the more than 700 resources in this booklet represent the growing field of information for and about children of acoholics. It is hoped that the information in this guide will assist you in your efforts. However, for children of alcoholics the greatest resource for recovery may be themselves and those who care about them.

ACKNOWLEDGMENT

Thanks to
Georgia M. Springer,
Research Assistant

DEDICATION

To

The Founding Members of

The National Association for Children of Alcoholics

CONTENTS

BOOKS

Abel, Ernest L. **Fetal Alcohol Syndrome and Fetal Alcohol Effects.** Research Institute on Alcoholism, Buffalo, NY, 1984.

Ackerman, R. J. **Same House, Different Homes.** Health Communications, Pompano Beach, FL 1987.

Ackerman, R. J. (editor) **Growing in the Shadow.** Health Communications, Pompano Beach, FL, 1986.

Ackerman, R. J. **Children of Alcoholics: Bibliography and Resource Guide** (3rd edition). Health Communications, Pompano Beach, FL, 1987.

Ackerman, R. J. **Children of Alcoholics: A Guide Book for Educators, Therapists, and Parents** (2nd edition). Learning Publications, Holmes Beach, FL, 1983.

Al-Anon Faces Alcoholism. Al-Anon Family Group Headquarters, New York, NY.

Al-Anon Family Groups. Al-Anon Family Group Headquarters, New York, NY.

Alateen: Hope for Children of Alcoholics. Al-Anon Family Group Headquarters, Inc., New York, NY, 1980.

Alateen — A Day At A Time. Al-Anon Family Group Headquarters, New York, NY, 1984.

Anonymous. **This New Day.** Quotidian Publications, Rockaway, NJ, 1985.

Barnard, Charles P. **Families, Alcoholism and Therapy.** Thomas Books, IL, 1981.

Bepko, Claudia. **The Responsibility Trap: A Blueprint for Treating the Alcoholic Family.** Free Press, New York, 1985.

Black, Claudia. **It Will Never Happen to Me.** Medical Administration Company, Denver, CO, 1982.

Black, Claudia. **My Dad Loves Me, My Dad Has A Disease.** Medical Administration Company, Denver, CO, 1982.

Black, Claudia. **Repeat After Me.** Medical Administration Company, Denver, CO, 1985.

Brennan, Gale P. **I Know They Love Me Anyway.** De Paul Rehabilitation Hospital, Milwaukee, WI, 1986.

Brenner, Avis. **Helping Children Cope with Stress.** Lexington Books, Lexington, MA, 1984.

Brooks, Cathleen. **The Secret Everyone Knows.** The Kroc Foundation, San Diego, CA, 1981.

Changing Legacies: Growing Up In An Alcoholic Home, Health Communications, Pompano Beach, FL, 1984.

Cork, Margaret R. **The Forgotten Children.** Addiction Research Foundation, Ontario, Canada, 1969.

Curtin, Paul. **Tumbleweeds: A Therapists' Guide to the Treatment of Adult Children of Alcoholics.** Quotidian Publications, Rockaway, NJ, 1985.

Deutsch, Charles. **Broken Bottles, Broken Dreams: Understanding and Helping the Children of Alcoholics.** Teachers College Press, Columbia University, New York, 1982.

Drews, T. R. **Getting Them Sober.** Bridge Publishing, Inc., South Plainfield, NJ, 1980.

Elkin, Michael. **Families Under the Influence: Changing Alcoholic Patterns.** W.W. Norton, New York, NY, 1984.

Felsen, Judy. **Reflections.** Quotidian Publications, Rockaway, NJ, 1987.

Forrest, Gary G. **How To Live With a Problem Drinker and Survive.** Atheneum Press, New York, 1980.

Fox, Ruth. **The Effect of Alcoholism on Children.** National Council on Alcoholism, New York, 1972.

Ginnott, H. **Between Parent and Child.** Avon Books, 1973.

Goldman, W. **The Color of Light.** Warner Books, New York, NY, 1984.

Goldberg, L. A. **Counseling Activities for Children of Alcoholics.** Apalachee Community Mental Health Services, Tallahassee, FL, 1983.

Goodwin, D. **Is Alcoholism Hereditary?** Oxford University Press, New York, 1976.

Gravitz, H. and J. Bowden. **Guide to Recovery: A Book for Adult Children of Alcoholics.** Learning Publications, Inc., Holmes Beach, FL, 1985.

Greenleaf, Jael. **Co-Alcoholic, Para-Alcoholic.** Jael Greenleaf, Los Angeles, CA, 1981.

Hansen, P. L. **Alcoholism: The Afflicted and Affected.** Graphic Publishing Company, Lake Mills, IA, 1974.

Harwin, J. and J. Orford. **Alcohol and the Family.** Croom Helm, England, 1980.

Hastings, J. M. **An Elephant in the Living Room: The Children's Book.** CompCare Publications, Minneapolis, MN, 1983.

Hastings, J.M. and M.H. Typpo. **An Elephant in the Living Room: A Guide for Working with Children of Alcoholics.** CompCare Publications, Minneapolis, MN 1983.

Heckler, Jonellen. **A Fragile Peace.** G. P. Putnam's Sons, New York, 1985.

Hornik, E. L. **You and Your Alcoholic Parent.** Association Press, New York, 1974.

Hornik-Beer, E. **A Teenager's Guide to Living with an Alcoholic Parent.** Hazelden, Center City, MN, 1984.

Jackson, J. **The Adjustment of the Family to the Crisis of Alcoholism.** National Council on Alcoholism, New York, 1954.

Johnson, V. E. **I'll Quit Tomorrow.** Harper and Row, New York, NY, 1980.

Jones, P. **The Brown Bottle.** Hazelden, Center City, MN, 1985.

Kaufman, E. and P. Kaufmann. **Family Therapy of Drug and Alcohol Abuse.** Gardner Press, New York, NY, 1979.

Keller, J. E. **Alcohol: A Family Affair.** The Kroc Foundation, San Diego, CA, 1977.

Keniston, K. and The Carnegie Council on Children. **All Our Children: The American Family Under Pressure.** Harcourt, Brace and Jovanovich, New York, 1977.

Kritsberg, Wayne. **The Adult Children of Alcoholics Syndrome: From Discovery to Recovery.** Health Communications, Pompano Beach, FL, 1986.

Lawson, Gary. **Alcoholism and the Family.** Aspen Publishers, Rockville, MD, 1983.

Lerner, Rokelle. **Daily Affirmations: For Adult Children of Alcoholics.** Health Communications, Pompano Beach, FL, 1985.

Lewis, David C., and Carol N. Williams. **Providing Care for Children of Alcoholics: Clinical and Research Perspectives.** Health Communications, Pompano Beach, FL, 1986.

Maxwell, M.A. **AA (Alcoholics Anonymous) Experience.** McGraw-Hill Book Co., New York, NY, 1984.

McConnell, Patty. **Adult Children of Alcoholics: A Workbook for Healing.** Harper and Row, San Francisco, CA, 1986.

Melquist, E. L. **Pepper.** Frederick County Council on Alcoholism, Frederick, MD, 1974.

McLachlan, J. and R. Waldeman and S. Thomas. **A Study of Teenagers with Alcoholic Parents.** The Donwood Institute, Toronto, Canada, 1973.

Mehl, D. **You and the Alcoholic in Your Home.** Augsberg, Minneapolis, MN, 1979.

Middelton-Moz, Jane and Lorie Dwinell. **After the Tears: Multigenerational Grief in Alcoholic Families.** Health Communications, Pompano Beach, FL, 1986.

Minot, S. **Monkeys.** E.P. Dutton/Seymour Lawrence, New York, NY, 1986.

Morehouse, Ellen R. **Preventing Alcohol Problems Through a Student Assistance Program.** NIAAA, Rockville, MD, 1984.

Mumey, J. **Sitting in the Bay Window.** Contemporary Books, Inc., Chicago, IL, 1984.

Norwood, Robin. **Women Who Love Too Much.** St. Martin's Press, New York, 1985.

Porterfield, K. M. **Coping with an Alcoholic Parent.** 1985.

Russell, Marcia, C. Henderson and S. Blume. **Children of Alcoholics: A Review of the Literature.** Children of Alcoholics Foundation, New York, NY, 1985.

Ryerson, E. **When Your Parent Drinks Too Much: A Book for Teenagers.** 1985.

Scales, Cynthia G. **Potato Chips For Breakfast: An Autobiography.** Quotidian Publications, Rockaway, NJ, 1986.

Scott, E. **Struggles in an Alcoholic Family.** Thomas Books, Illinois, 1970.

Seixas, J.S. and G. Youcha. **Children of Alcoholism: A Survivor's Manual.** Crown Publishers, New York, NY, 1985.

Seixas, J. S. **Living with a Parent Who Drinks Too Much.** Greenwillow Press, New York, NY, 1979.

Smith, B. **A Tree Grows in Brooklyn.** Harper and Row, New York, NY, 1947.

Subby, R. **Lost in The Shuffle.** Health Communications, Pompano Beach, FL, 1987.

Tessmer, K., **Breaking the Silence: A Workbook for Adult COA** A.C.A.T. Press, Santa Rosa, CA, 1986.

Thompson, C. and L. Rudolph. **Counseling Children.** Brooks/Cole Publishing Company, Monterey, CA, 1983.

Van Ornum, W. and J. Mordock. **Crisis Counseling with Children and Adolescents.** Continuum Publishing Company, New York, NY, 1983.

Wegscheider, Sharon and Esterly, R.W., **Alcoholism and the Family: A Book of Readings.** Caron Institute, Wernersville, PA, 1985.

Wegscheider, Sharon. **A Second Chance.** Science and Behavior Books, Palo Alto, CA, 1980.

Wegscheider, Sharon. **Another Chance: Hope and Health for the Alcoholic Family.** Science and Behavior Books, Palo Alto, CA, 1981.

Wegscheider-Cruse, Sharon. **Choicemaking.** Health Communications, Pompano Beach, FL, 1985.

Wegscheider-Cruse, Sharon. **Learning to Love Yourself.** Health Communications, Pompano Beach, FL, 1987.

Wegscheider-Cruse, Sharon. **Understanding Me.** Health Communications, Pompano Beach, FL, 1986.

Wisniewski, Rita. **I Know They Love Me Anyway: Utilization Guidebook for Teachers, Counselors, Parents.** De Paul Rehabilitation Hospital, Milwaukee, WI, 1986.

Whitfield, Charles. **Healing the Child Within.** Health Communications, Pompano Beach, FL, 1987.

Woititz, Janet G. **The Struggle for Intimacy.** Health Communications, Pompano Beach, FL, 1985.

Woititz, Janet G. **Adult Children of Alcoholics.** Health Communications, Pompano Beach, FL, 1983.

Woititz, Janet G. **Home Away From Home.** Health Communications, Pompano Beach, FL, 1987.

Zimberg, Sheldon, and Wallace, John, and Blume, Sheila. **Practical Approaches to Alcoholism Psychotherapy** (2nd Edition) Plenum Press, New York, NY, 1985.

RESEARCH AND ARTICLES

Ackerman, R. J. "The Denial of Other Victims". **The Domino Quarterly,** Spring/Summer, 1983.

Ackerman, R. J. "Alcoholism in the Family" in Robert J. Ackerman(ed) **Growing in the Shadow,** Health Communications, Pompano Beach, FL, 1986.

Ackerman, R. J. "Alcoholic Parents: Reducing the Impact". **Focus on Family and Chemical Dependency,** Vol.7(1), Jan/Feb 1984.

Ackerman, R. J. "Alcoholism and the Family" in **New Perspectives on Alcoholism,** University of Akron Medical School, 1983.

Adler R. and B. Raphael. "Children of Alcoholics". **Australian and New Zealand Journal of Psychiatry,** 17, 1, 3, 1983.

Aldoory, S. "Research into Family Factors in Alcoholism" **Alcohol and Research World,** Summer, 1979, 3, 2-6.

Allen, T. "Adolescent Substance Abuse and the Role of Families, Schools and Communities" in Robert J. Ackerman (ed.) **Growing in'the Shadow,** Health Communications, Pompano Beach, FL, 1986.

Alterman, A.I. and R. Tarter. "Role of Alcohol in Family Violence". Veteran's Administration Medical Center, **Journal of Studies on Alcohol,** 46(3):256-258, 1985.

Anderson, P. "Recovery is Child's Play." **Alcoholism,** Vol. 4(7), Dec 1983.

Anderson, S. "Working with Black Adult Children of Alcoholics" in Robert J. Ackerman (ed.) **Growing in the Shadow,** Health Communications, Pompano Beach, FL, 1986.

Archer, N. S. "Perceptions and Attitudes of Family Members (Co-Dependents), Pre and Post Treatment". **Labor Management Alcoholism Journal,** 1979, 9(2), 75-80.

Arentzen, W. P. "Impact of Alcohol Misuse on Family Life" **Alcoholism: Clinical and Experimental Research,** 1978, 2 (4), 349-351.

Aronson, H. and A. Gilbert. "Pre-Adolescent Sons of Male Alcoholics". **Archives of General Psychiatry,** 1963, 8, 235-241.

Aronson, M. et al. "Children of Alcoholic Mothers: Developmental, Perceptual and Behavioral Characteristics as Compared to Matched Controls". **Acta Paediatrica Scandinavica** 74:27-34,1985. Atkins, M. "A Family Approach to the Treatment of Alcoholism". Paper presented at National Conference on Social Welfare, Dallas, TX, 1971.

Balcerzak, J. G. "Children of Alcoholics: A Review and Clinical Observations". **Michigan Journal on Women and Alcohol,** 1978.

Balis, S. "Illusions that Affect Treatment for Adult Children of Alcoholics". **Focus on Family and Chemical Dependency,** 8(3), 16-17, 1985.

Bard, M. and J. Zacker. "Assaultiveness and Alcohol Use in Family Disputes". **Criminology,** 1974, 12(3), 281-292.

Barlow, B. "The School's Role in Helping Children of Alcoholics". **Focus on Family and Chemical Dependency,** Vol. 7(2), Mar/Apr 1984.

Barnes, G. M. "The Development of Adolescent Drinking Behavior: An Evaluative Review of the Impact of the Socialization Process Within the Family". **Adolescence,** 1977, 12(48), 571-591.

Barnes, J. L. and C. S. Benson. "Psychological Characteristics of Women with Alcoholic Fathers". **Currents in Alcoholism,** 1979, 6(6), 209-222.

Barr, H.M. et al. "Infant Size at 8 Months of Age: Relationship to Maternal Use of Alcohol, Nicotine and Caffeine During Pregnancy". **Pediatrics,** 74:336-341, 1984.

Behling, D. W. "Alcohol Abuse as Encountered in 51 Instances of Reported Child Abuse". **Clinical Pediatrics,** 1979, 18(2), 87-91.

Bennett, L.A. "Combining Qualitative and Quantitative Methods in Studies of Familial Alcoholism". **Drinking and Drug Surveyor,** (20):5-52, 1985.

Benson, C.G. "Coping and Support Among Daughters of Alcoholics". Unpublished doctoral dissertation. Indiana University, 1980.

Biek, J. E. "Screening Test for Identifying Adolescents Adversely Affected by a Parental Drinking Problem". **Journal of Adolescent Health Care,** 1981, 2, 107-113.

Black, C. "Community Must Accept Responsiblity". **Focus on Alcohol and Drug Issues,** Vol. 6(2), Mar/Apr 1983, 13, 25.

Black, C. "Children of Alcoholics". **Catalyst,** 1980, 1(3), 5-21.

Black, C. "Children of Alcoholics". **Alcohol Health and Research World,** 1979, 4, 23-27.

Black, C. "Innocent Bystanders at Risk: The Children of Alcoholics". **Alcoholism,** 1981, 1(3), 22-26.

Black, C. "Children of Alcoholics", **Alcohol Health and Research World** 4(1)23:27, 1979. National Clearing-house for Alcohol Information, Rockville, MD.

Black, C. "CoA's: The Clinical Profile". **Focus on Family and Chemical Dependency,** Vol. 6(6), Nov/Dec 1983.

Black, C. and S. Brown, "Kids of Alcoholics". **Newsweek,** May, 1979.

Black, C. "Teaching, Talking, Touching". **Alcoholism: The National Magazine,** 5(2) 26-28, 1984.

Black, C. Bucky, S. & Wilder-Padilla. "The Interpersonal and Emotional Consequences of Being an Adult Child of an Alcoholic". **The International Journal of the Addictions,** 21(2),213-231, 1986.

√ Blanchard, J.M. "Psychological Profiles of Children of Alcoholics: Self-Concept and Leisure Attitude", University of Colorado, Boulder, CO, Dissertation Abstracts International 45(3A): 9611, 1984.

Booz-Allen and Hamilton. "An Assessment of the Needs of and Resources for the Children of Alcoholic Parents" NIAAA Contract Report, 1974.

Booz-Allen and Hamilton. "Final Report on the Needs of and Resources for Children of Alcoholic Parents". Rockville, MD, NIAAA, 1974.

Bonk, J.R., "Perceptions of Psychodynamics During a Transitional Period as Reported in Families Affected by Alcoholism". University of Arizona, Tucson, Dissertation Abstracts International, 46(2): 634B, 1985.

Bosma, W. G. H. "Children of Alcoholics — A Hidden Tragedy". **Maryland State Medical Journal,** 1972, 21(1), 34-36.

Boureois, M., Levigne, O. and H. Pelage. "Children of Alcoholics: Survey of 66 Children of Alcoholics in a Child Psychiatry Service". **Annales Medico-Psychologiques,** 1975, 2(3), 592-609.

Bowels, C. "Children of Alcoholic Parents". **American Journal of Nursing,** 1968, 68(5), 1062-1064.

Bowen, M. "A Family Systems Approach to Alcoholism". **Addictions,** 1974, 21(2).

Brooks, C. "Beyond the Pain: Children of Alcoholics Do Recover". **Focus on Family and Chemical Dependency,** Vol. 7(2), Mar/Apr 1984.

Brooks, K. "Adult Children of Alcoholics: Psychosocial Stages of Development". **Focus on Family and Chemical Dependency,** Vol. 6(5), Sept/Oct 1983.

Brown, K. and J. Sunshine. "Group Treatment of Children of Alcoholic Families". In M. Altman and R. Crocker (eds.), **Social Groupwork and Alcoholism.** Haworth Press, NY, 1982.

Brown, S. "Personality Characteristics of the Teenage Daughters of Male Alcoholics". Masters Thesis, San Jose State University, 1974.

Brown, S. and S. Beletsis. "The Development of Family Transference for Adult Children of Alcoholics". **International Journal of Group Psychotherapy,** 1985.

Burk, E. "Some Contemporary Issues in Child Development and Children of Alcoholic Parents". **Annals of the New York Academy of Sciences,** May 1972, 1987, 189.

Cadoret, R. and A. Gath. "Inheritance of Alcoholism in Adoptees". **British Journal of Psychiatry,** 132, 252-258, 1978.

Cadoret, R. et al. "Development of Alcoholism in Adoptees Raised Apart from Alcoholic Biologic Relatives". **Archives of General Psychiatry,** 37, 561-563, 1980.

Callan, V. and D. Jackson. "Children of Alcoholic Fathers: Recovered Alcoholic Fathers, Personal and Family Functioning". **Journal of Studies on Alcohol,** 47, 2, 180, 1986.

Caplan, R. "Dependency and Dependency Conflict in Offspring of Problem Drinking Parents". Dissertation Abstracts International, 44(06), 19533-8, 1983.

Carey, P. and B. B. "It Will Never Happen to Me. The Grown-up Employed Child of the Alcoholic. Implications for the Industrial Alcoholism Field". Presented at ALMACA Convention, 1979.

Caution, G. "Alcoholism and the Black Family". In Robert J. Ackerman (ed.) **Growing in the Shadow,** Health Communications, Pompano Beach, FL, 1986.

Cermak, T. "Children of Alcoholics and the Case for a New Diagnostic Category of Co-Dependency". **Alcohol Health and Research World,** Vol. 8(4), Summer 1984, 38-42.

Cermak, T. "The Birth of NACoA". **Focus on Family and Chemical Dependency,** Vol. 6(5), Sept/Oct 1983.

Cermak, T. "Reality and Power: Treating Children of Alcoholics". **Focus on Family and Chemical Dependency,** Vol. 7(2), Mar/Apr 1984.

Cermak, T. "Parallels in the Recovery Process for Alcoholics and Adult Children of Alcoholics". Paper presented at the National Council on Alcoholism Forum, Houston, TX, 1983.

Cermak, T. L. and S. Brown. "Interactional Group Therapy with the Adult Children of Alcoholics". **International Journal of Group Psychotherapy,** 1982, 32(3), 375-389.

Chafetz, M. E. "Children of Alcoholics". **New York University Education Quarterly,** 1979, 10(3), 23-39.

Chafetz, M. E., Blane, H. and M. J. Hill. "Children of Alcoholics: Observations in a Child Guidance Clinic". **Quarterly Journal of Studies on Alcohol,** 1971, 32, 687-698.

"Children of Alcoholics Learn to Make Choices". Children of Alcoholics: A Special Report. National Insitute on Alcohol Abuse and Alcoholism, January 1984.

"Children of Alcoholics: An Interview with the NIAAA Director". **Alcohol Health and Research World,** Vol. 8(4), Summer 1984, 3-5.

Church, M. "Hearing Loss Among FAS Children". **The U. S. Journal of Drug & Alcohol Dependence,** Vol. 8(9), Sept 1984, 19.

Claire, D. & M. Genest. "Variables Associated with the Adjustment of Offspring of Alcoholic Fathers." Paper presented at the Annual Convention of the American Psychological Association (92nd), Toronto, Canada, August, 1984.

Clarren, S. and D. Smith. "The Fetal Alcohol Syndrome: A Review of the World Literature". **New England Journal of Medicine,** 1978, 298, 1063-1067.

Corder, B.F., McRee, C., and Rohrer, H. "Brief Review of Literature on Daughters of Alcoholic Fathers". **North Carolina Journal of Mental Health** 10(20):37-43, 1984.

Cork, R.M. "The Forgotten Children: A Study of Children with Alcoholic Parents". Toronto: Alcoholism Foundation of Ontario, Canada 1969. Update, Alcohol Clin. Res. 3:148-157, 1979.

Cotton, N. S. "The Familial Incidence of Alcoholism". **Journal of Alcohol Studies,** 1979, 40, 89-112.

Count, E. "28 Million Forgotten Children: Help for Young Victims of Alcoholic Homes". **Family Circle,** December, 1976.

√ Cramer, P. A. "An Educational Strategy to Impact the Children of Alcoholic Parents: A Feasibility Report". National Center for Alcohol Education, March, 1977.

Cutter, H. and J. Fisher. "Family Experience and the Motives for Drinking". **International Journal of the Addictions,** 1980, 15(3), 339-358.

Cutter, C. "How Do People Change in Al-Anon? Reports of Adult Children of Alcoholics". Dissertation Abstracts International, 46(7), 2087A-2088A, 1986.

Dalton, J. and M. West. "Mothers, Children Together — A New Approach for Eagleville," **Focus,** 1979, 2(3), 6-7.

Darby, B.L., Streissguth, A.P., and Smith, D.W. "A Preliminary Follow-up of 8 Children Diagnosed Fetal Alcohol Syndrome in Infancy". **Neurobehavioral Toxicology and Teratology** 3:157 159, 1981.

Davis, A., and Lipson, A. "A Challenge in Managing a Family with the Fetal Alcohol Syndrome". Letter in Clinical Pediatrics 23:304, 1984.

Davis, D. "The Family in Alcoholism". In **Phenomenology and Treatment of Alcoholism.** Spectrum Publications, New York, 1980.

Davis, T. and L. Hagood. "In-Home Support for Recovering Alcoholic Mothers and Their Families: The Family Rehabilitation Project". **Journal of Studies on Alcohol,** 1979, 40(3), 313-317.

Deckman, J. and B. Downs. "Group Treatment Approach for Adolescent Children of Alcoholic Parents". In M. Altman and R. Crocker (eds.) **Social Groupwork and Alcoholism.** Haworth Press, New York, 1982.

Deutsch, C. "Planning Community-Based Services". **Focus on Alcohol and Drug Issues,** Vol. 6(2), Mar/Apr 1983, 5-7.

Deutsch, C. "The Surprise in Pandora's Box: Teachers Help Children with Family Alcoholism". Paper presented at the annual meeting of the National Council on Alcoholism, 1979.

Deutsch, C., DiCicco, L. and D. Mills. "Services for Children of Alcoholic Parents". Presented at the 29th Annual Meeting Alcohol and Drug Programs Association of North America, 1978.

Deutsch, C., DiCicco, L. and D. Mills. "Children of Parents with Alcoholism". National Institute on Alcohol Abuse and Alcoholism, 1980.

Deutsch, C., DiCicco, L. and D. Mills. "Prevention, Intervention and Treatment: Concerns and Models". **NIAAA Alcohol and Health Monograph No. 3,** DHHS Pub. N. ADM 82-1192, U.S. Government Printing Office, 1982.

Deutsch, C., DiCicco, L. and D. Mills. "Prevention, Intervention and Treatment: Concerns and Models". **NIAAA Alcohol and Health Monograph No. 3,** DHHS Pub. N. ADM 82-1192, U.S. Government Printing Office, 1982.

Diaz, P. "Reaching Hispanic Children of Alcoholics in Their Own Community" Paper presented at the National Council on Alcoholism Annual Forum, 1982.

Diaz, P. and J. Slotwinski. "Helping Children to Help Themselves". **Focus on Family and Chemical Dependency,** Vol. 7(2), Mar/Apr 1984.

Diaz, P. "Self Help Groups: Through the Children's Eyes", **Focus on Family and Chemical Dependency,** 8(2), 28029, 1985.

Diaz, P. and R. Figueroa. "Hispanics and Alcoholism: A Treatment Perspective". in Robert J. Ackerman (ed.) **Growing in the Shadow,** Health Communications, Pompano Beach, FL, 1986.

DiCicco, et al. "Identifying the Children of Alcoholic Parents from Survey Responses". **Journal of Alcohol and Drug Education,** 30(1), 1-17, 1984.

DiCicco, L. et al. "Group Experiences for Children of Alcoholics". **Alcohol Health and Research World,** Vol. 8(4), Summer 1984, 20-24.

DiCicco, L. "Children of Alcoholic Parents: Issues in Identification". Paper presented at the NIAAA Symposium on Services to Children of Alcoholics, 1979.

Donovan, B. "Collegiate Groups for Sons and Daughters of Alcoholics". **Journal of the American College Health Association,** 1981, 30(2), 83-86.

Dulfano, C. "Recovery: Rebuilding the Family". **Alcoholism,** 1981, 1(3), 33-39.

el-Guebaly, N. "The Offspring of Alcoholics: Outcome Predictors". **Journal of Children in Contemporary Society,** 1982, 15(1), 3-12.

el-Guebaly, N. and D. Offord. "On Being the Offspring of an Alcoholic: An Update". **Alcoholism Clinical and Experimental Research,** 1979, 3(2), 148-157.

el-Guebaly, N. and D. Offord. "The Offspring of Alcoholics: A Critical Review". **American Journal of Psychiatry,** 1977, 134, (4), 357-364.

Elliot, D. and N. Johnson. "Fetal Alcohol Syndrome: Implications and Counseling Considerations". **Personal and Guidance Journal,** 1983, 62(2), 67-69.

Ellwood, L. "Effects on Alcoholism as a Family Illness on Child Behavior and Development". **Military Medicine,** 1980, 145(3).

Ervin, C.S. et al. "Alcoholic Fathering and Its Relation to Child's Intellectual Development: A Pilot Investigation". **Alcoholism: Clinical and Experimental Research** 8(4):362-365, 1984.

Evans, D.G. "Alcoholism, Domestic Violence and the Law." **Focus on Family** 8(5):10-11, 42-43, 1985.

Farber, D. "Families May Mask Alcoholism". Focus, 1981, 4(3), 25.

FAS/FAE Bibliography. "Alcohol and Pregnancy: Fetal Alcohol Syndrome and Fetal Alcohol Effects." Wisconsin Clearinghouse, P.O. Box 1468, Madison, WI, 53701.

"Fetal Effects of Moderate Drinking Persist in 8-Month-Olds", **Medical World News,** (New York) Nov. 1984.

Fine, E., et al. "Behavioral Disorders in Children with Parental Alcoholism". **Annals of the New York Academy of Sciences,** 1976, 23, 507-517.

Flanzer, J. P. "Alcohol Abusing Parents and Their Battered Adolescents". **Currents in Alcoholism,** 1979, 7, 529-539.

Flanzer, J. P. "Double Trouble: Alcoholism and Family Violence", in Robert J. Ackerman (ed.) **Growing in the Shadow,** Health Communication, Pompano Beach, FL, 1986

Foster, W. "The Employed Child of the Alcoholic". **Labor Management Journal,** 1976, 6(1), 13-18.

Fox, R. "Children in the Alcoholic Family". In Bier, W (ed.), Problems in Addiction: Alcohol and Drug Addiction. New York: Fordham Univ. Press, 1962, 71-96.

Fox, R. "Teaching the Alcoholic's Family" In R. Cantanzaro (ed.), **Alcoholism: The Total Treatment Approach** Thomas Books, IL, 1968.

Frances, R.J. et al. "Outcome Study of Familial and Nonfamilial Alcoholism". **American Journal of Psychiatry** 41(11): 1469-1471, 1984.

Gabrielli, W. et al. "Electroencephalograms in Children of Alcoholic Fathers". **Psychophysiology,** 19, 404-407, 1982.

Gabrielli, W. and S. Mednick. "Intellectual Performance in Children of Alcoholics". **Journal of Nervous and Mental Disease,** 171, 7, 444, 1983.

Gennett, S. "Daughters of Alcoholic Fathers: An Investigation of Personality Traits". Dissertation Abstracts International, 44(04), 1236-B, 1237-B, 1983.

Globetti, G. "Alcohol: A Family Affair". Paper presented at North American Congress of Parents and Teachers, 1973.

Gold, S. and L. Sherry. "Hyperactivity, Learning Disabilities, and Alcohol". **Journal of Learning Disabilities,** 1984, 17(1), 3-6.

Goldman, A.P. "Relationship of Alcoholic Mothers and Their Children: Description and Evaluation". Dissertation Abstracts International, 46(5):1685-B, 1985.

Goodwin, D. "Alcoholism and Genetics: The Sins of the Fathers". **Archives of General Psychiatry,** 42(2), 171-174, 1985.

Goodwin, D. "Adoption Studies of Alcoholism". **Journal of Operational Psychiatry,** 1976, 7(1), 54-63.

Goodwin, D. "Psychopathology in Adopted and Nonadopted Daughters of Alcoholics" **Archives of General Psychiatry,** 1977, 34(9), 1005-1009.

Goodwin, D. et al. "Drinking Problems in Adopted and Non-Adopted Sons of Alcoholics". **Archives of General Psychiatry,** 1974, 31(2), 164-169.

Goodwin, D. "The Genetics of Alcoholism: A State of the Art Review". **Alcohol Health and Research World,** Spring, 1978, 2(3), 2-12.

Goodwin, D. "The Genetics of Alcoholism", **Alcohol Technical Reports,** 12-13:7-11, 1983-84.

Goon, M. "If One of Your Parents Drinks Too Much, What are Your Problems Going to Be?". **Glamour,** October 1978.

Golden N.L.; Sokol, R.J.; Kunhert, B.R.; and Bottoms, B. "Maternal Alcohol Use and Infant Development". **Pediatrics,** 70:931-934, 1982.

Gorski, T. and M. Miller. "Relapse: The Family's Involvement". **Focus on Family and Chemical Dependency,** 6(5), 17-17, 1983.

Gravitz, H. and J. Bowden. "Therapeutic Issues of Adult Children of Alcoholics". **Alcohol Health and Research World,** Vol. 8(4), Summer 1984, 25-29.

Gravitz, H. and J. Bowden. "Recovery Continuum for Adult Children of Alcoholics: Insights to Treatment". **Focus on Family and Chemical Dependency,** 8(3), 1985.

Greenleaf, J. "What We Don't Know Can Hurt Us . . . And Others". **Focus on Alcohol and Drug Issues,** Vol. 6(2), Mar/Apr 1983, 14.

Gunderson, I. "Incest and Alcoholism". **Catalyst,** 1980, 1(3), 22-25.

Haberman, P. " Childhood Symptoms in Children of Alcoholics and Comparison Group Parents". **Journal of Marriage and the Family,** 1966, 28, 152-154.

Hanson, J. et al. "Fetal Alcohol Syndrome: Experience with 41 Patients". **Journal of the American Medical Association,** 1976, 235, 1458-1460.

Harrington, V. "A Family Disease". **Momentum,** 1983, 14(3), 28-30.

Harwood, H.J.; Napolitano, D.M., "Economic Implications of the Fetal Alcohol Syndrome", **Alcohol Health and Research World** 10(1):38-43, 74-75, 1985.

Hassett, C. "The Relationship of Gender, Alcoholic Parentage and Intervention to Mental Abilities, Locus of Control and Zinc Level". Dissertation Abstracts International, 1981, 42, 5-B, 2110.

Hawley, N., and E. Brown. "Use of Group Treatment with Children of Alcoholics". **Social Casework,** 1981, 62(1), 40-46.

Hecht, M. "Children of Alcoholics are Children at Risk". **American Journal of Nursing,** 1973, 73(10), 1746-1767.

Heller, K. et al. "Problems Associated with Risk Over Prediction in Studies of Offspring of Alcoholics: Implications for Prevention". **Clinical Psychology Review,** 1982, 2(2), 183-200.

"Helping Kids with Alcoholic Parents", **Boston Globe,** January 19, 1980.

Hennecke, L. "Stimulus Augmenting and Field Dependence in Children of Alcoholic Fathers". **Journal of Studies on Alcohol,** 45, 6, 486-492, 1984.

Herjanic, B. et al. "Children of Alcoholics". in Seixas, F. (ed.). **Currents in Alcoholism,** Vol. II, New York: Grune & Stratton, 1977, 445-455.

Hindeman, M. "Children of Alcoholic Parents". Alcohol Health and Research World, Winter, 1975-76.

Hindeman, M. "Child Abuse and Neglect: The Alcohol Connection". Alcohol Health and Research World, 1977, 1(3).

Hindeman, M. "Research on Children of Alcoholics: Expanding the Knowledge". **Alcohol Health and Research World,** 1984, 8, (4).

Holzman, I. "Fetal Alcohol Syndrome (FAS) — A Review". **Journal of Children in Contemporary Society,** 1982, 15(1), 13-19.

Homonoff, E. and A. Stephen. "Alcohol Education for Children of Alcoholics in a Boston Neighborhood". **Journal of Studies on Alcohol,** 1979, 40, 923-926.

Horowitz, S. "Fetal Alcohol Effects in Children: Cognitive, Educational, and Behavioral Considerations". Paper presented Annual International Convention Council for Exceptional Children, 1983.

Huber, K.E. "Comparison of Adolescents from Alcoholic And Non-Alcoholic Families". United States International University, San Diego, CA. Dissertation Abstracts International 45(1): 3321B, 1985.

Hughes, J. "Adolescent Children of Alcoholic Parents and the Relationship of Alateen to These Children". **Journal of Consulting and Clinical Psychology,** 1977, 45(5), 946-947.

Ingram, C.R. "Adult Children of Alcoholics: The Issues in Their Lives", University of San Francisco, San Francisco, CA, Dissertation Abstracts International, 46(5) 1688B, 1985.

Jackson, J. "Alcoholism and The Family". In D. Pittman and C, Snyder (eds.), **Society, Culture, and Drinking Patterns.** John Wiley, New York, 1962.

Jackson, J.G., "Personality Characteristics of Adult Daughters of Alcoholic Fathers as Compared With Adult Daughters of Non-Alcoholic Fathers". United States International University, San Diego, CA, Dissertation Abstracts International 46(1): 338-B, 1985.

Jacob, T. "An Introduction to the Alcoholic's Family" **Currents in Alcoholism,** 1980, 7, 505-513.

Jacob, T. et al. "The Alcoholic's Spouse, Children, and Family Interactions". **Journal of Studies on Alcohol.** 1978, 39, 1231-1251.

Jones, J. "Ways to Use the C.A.S.T.". Family Recovery Press, Chicago, IL, 1982.

Jones, K.L. et al. "Outcome in Offspring of Chronic Alcoholic Women". **Lancet,** 1974, 1, 1076-1078.

Jurich, A. et al. "Family Factors in the Lives of Drug Users and Abusers". **Adolescence,** 1985, 20(77), 143-159.

Kammeier, M.L. "Adolescents from Families with and without Alcohol Problems". **Quarterly Journal of Studies on Alcohol,** 1971, 32, 364-372.

Katunich, Karen Louise. "Learned Helplessness in Children of Alcoholics", Virginia Commonwealth University, 1984.

Kearney, T. and C. Taylor. "Emotionally Disturbed Adolescents with Alcoholic Parents". **Acta Paedopsychiatra,** 36(6 & 7), 215-221.

Kern, J. "Adult Children of Alcoholics as Professionals in the Alcoholism Field" in Robert J. Ackerman (ed.) **Growing in the Shadow,** Health Communications, Pompano Beach, FL, 1986.

Kern, J. et al. "Children of Alcoholics: Locus of Control, Mental Age, and Zinc Level". **Journal of Psychiatric Treatment and Evaluation,** 1981, 3(2), 169-173.

Kern, J. et al. "A Treatment Approach for Children of Alcoholics". **Journal of Drug Education,** 1977-78, 7, 207-218.

Kim, Y.C. "Studies on Familial Alcoholism: A Review". **Journal of Experimental Education,** 52(3), 163-167, 1984.

King, B. "Betraying the Alcoholic or Protecting the Child: The Dilemma of Confidentiality". **Alcoholism,** 3(7), 59-61, 1983.

Knight, J. "Family in the Crisis of Alcoholism". In S. Gitlow and H. Peyser (eds.), **Alcoholism: A Practical Treatment Guide.** Grune and Stratton, New York, 1980.

Korcok, M. "The Founding, Future, and Vision of NACoA". **The U.S. Journal of Drug and Alcohol Dependence,** Vol. 7(12), Dec. 1983, 19.

Korcok, M. "Alcoholism is a Family Affair". **Focus on Alcohol and Drug Issues,** May/June, 1979, 2, 4.

Krauthamer, C. "Maternal Attitudes of Alcoholic and Nonalcoholic Upper Middle Class Women". **The International Journal of the Addictions,** 1979, 14(5), 639-644.

Krimmel, H. "The Alcoholic and His Family". In P. Bourne and R. Fox (eds.), **Alcoholism: Progress in Research and Treatment.** Academic Press, New York, 1973.

Kritsberg, W. "The Family Tree". **Focus on Family and Chemical Dependency,** Vol. 6(5), Sept/Oct 1983.

Kritsberg, W. "Chronic Shock and Emotional Numbness in Adult Children of Alcoholics" **Focus on Family and Chemical Dependency,** Vol. 7(6), 1984.

Kyllerman, M. et al. "Children of Alcoholic Mothers: Growth and Motor Performance Compared to Matched Controls". **Acta Paediatrica Scandinavica,** 1985, 74, 20-26.

Landesman-Dwyer, et al. "Naturalistic Observation of Newborns: Effects of Maternal Alcohol Intake". **Alcoholism: Clinical and Experimental Research,** 1978, 2, 171-177.

Landesman-Dwyer, S. "Relationship of Children's Behavior to Maternal Alcohol Consumption". In E. Abel (ed.), **Human Studies, Fetal Alcohol Syndrome.** Vol. 2., CRC Press, Inc., Boca Raton, FL, 1982.

Lanier, D. "Familial Alcoholism". **Journal of Family Practice,** 18(3), 417-422, 1984.

Latcham, R. W. "Familial Alcoholism: Evidence from 237 Alcoholics". **British Journal of Psychiatry,** 1985, 147, 54-57.

Laudinet, S. and C. Kohler. "New Reflections on the Descent of Alcoholic Parents". **Psychiatrie de l'Enfant,** 1970, 13(1), 273-305.

Lawson, G. and A. Lawson. "Treating the Whole Family: When Intervention and Education Aren't Enough". **Focus on Family and Chemical Dependency,** Vol. 7(4), July/Aug 1984.

Lerner, R. "Schools Can Provide Drug Abuse Prevention Tools". **Focus on Alcohol and Drug Issues,** Vol. 6(2), Mar/Apr 1983, 22-23.

Lerner, R. "Laughter, Creativity and Play — Letting the Child Out". **Focus on Family and Chemical Dependency,** Vol. 7(2), Mar/Apr 1984.

Liepman, M. "Some Theoretical Connections Between Family Violence and Substance Abuse". **Catalyst,** 1980, 1(3), 37-42.

Liepman, M. et al. "Family Oriented Treatment of Alcoholism". **Rhode Island Medical Journal,** 1985, 68(3), 123-126.

Lindbeck, V. "The Adjustment of Adolescents to Paternal Alcoholism". Paper presented at Massachusetts General Hospital, Boston, April, 1971.

Lipscomb, W. and L. Goddard. "Black Family Features and Drinking Behavior". **Journal of Drug Issues,** 14(2):337-347, 1984.

Longie, J. "Alcohol and American Indian Children: An Assessment of Attitudes and Behavior". **Dissertation Abstracts International,** 44(11):3228-A, 1984.

Lovinfosse, M. "Incest Connection". **Alcoholism: The National Magazine,** 5(2), 51, 1984.

Lund, C. and S. Landesman-Dwyer. "Pre-Delinquent and Disturbed Adolescents: The Role of Parental Alcoholism". **Currents in Alcoholism,** 1978, 5, 339-348, 1978.

Manning, D. and B. Manning. "Bibliotherapy for Children of Alcoholics". **Journal of Reading,** 1984, 27(8), 720-25.

Marcus, A. "Comparative Study of Maternal Alcoholism and Maternal Child-Rearing Attitudes, Child Perception of Maternal Behavior, Child's Academic Achievement and School Attendance". **Dissertation Abstracts International,** 44(07), 2267-8, 1984.

Marcus, A. "Academic Achievement in Elementary School Children of Alcoholic Mothers". **Journal of Clinical Psychology,** 42(2), 372-376, 1986.

Marcus, A. "Comparative Study of Maternal Alcoholism and Maternal Child-Rearing Attitudes, Child Perception of Maternal Behavior, Child's Academic Achievement and School Attendance". Dissertation Abstracts International, 44(07), 2267B, 1984.

Martin, J.C. and G. L. Kirchner. "Attention and Distraction at Age 7 Years Related to Maternal Drinking During Pregnancy". **Alcoholism: Clinical and Experiential Research,** 1985, 9, 195.

Mason, V. G. "Reaching the Native American Children of Alcoholic Families". Paper presented at the National Council on Alcoholism Annual Forum, 1982.

Mayer, J. and R. Black. "The Relationship Between Alcoholism and Child Abuse and Neglect". **Currents in Alcoholism,** 1977, 4, 429-444.

✓ McAndrew, J. "Children of Alcoholics: School Intervention". **Childhood Education,** May/June, 343-345, 1985.

McCabe, J. "Children in Need: Consent Issues in Treatment". **Alcohol and Research World,** 1977, 2(1).

McCabe, J. "Many Children of Alcoholics Overcome Difficulties". **U.S. Journal of Drug and Alcohol Dependence,** 1981, 5(3), 6.

McDarby, D. "Children of the Damned: Alcoholic Children of Alcoholics". **Drug Survival News,** Vol. 9(1), July/August 1980.

McDonald, J. "Social Work in Family Life Enrichment: The Children of Alcoholics — A Montessori Approach". **American Montessori Society Bulletin,** 1978, 16(1), 1-14.

McKenna, T. and R. Pickens. "Alcoholic Children of Alcoholics". **Journal of Studies on Alcohol,** 1981, 42(11), 1021-1029.

McKenna, T. and R. Pickens. "Personality Characteristics of Alcoholic Children of Alcoholics". **Journal of Studies on Alcohol,** 44(4), 688-700, 1983.

Meeks, D. and C. Kelly. "Family Therapy with the Families of Recovering Alcoholics". **Quarterly Journal of Studies on Alcohol,** 1970, 31(2), 399-413.

Mendonca, M. "Pedopsychiatric Study of the Children of Alcoholic Parents". **Revue de Neuropsychiatrie Infantile et d'Hygiene Mentale de l'Enfance,** 1977, 25(7), 411-428.

Merikangas, K.R. et al. "Familial Transmission of Depression and Alcoholism". **Archives of General Psychiatry** 42(4): 367-372, 1985.

Middelton-Moz, Jane. "The Wisdom of Elders: Working with Native American and Alaskan Families". in Robert J. Ackerman (ed.) **Growing in the Shadow,** Health Communications, Pompano Beach, FL, 1986.

Middelton-Moz, Jane and L. Dwinell. "After the Tear: Working Through Grief, Loss, and Depression with Adult Children of Alcoholics". in Robert J. Ackerman (ed.) **Growing in the Shadow,** Health Communications, Pompano Beach, FL, 1986.

Miller, D., and Jang, M., "Children of Alcoholics: A 20-Year Longitudinal Study". Paper presented at the International Symposium on Alcohol and Drug Dependence, Tokyo, Japan, Aug. 23, 1977.

Miller, S. & B. Tuchfeld. "Adult Children of Alcoholics". **Hospital and Community Psychiatry,** 37, 3, 235-240, 1986.

Moos, R. and A. Billings. "Children of Alcoholics During the Recovery Process: Alcoholics and Matched Control Families". **Addictive Behaviors,** 1982, 7(2), 155-163.

✓ Moos, R. et al. "Family Characteristics and the Outcome of Treatment for Alcoholism". **Journal of Studies on Alcohol,** 1979, 40(1), 78-88.

✓ Morehouse, Ellen R. "Working with Adolescent Children of Alcoholics". In Robert J. Ackerman (ed.) **Growing in the Shadow,** Health Communications, Pompano Beach, FL, 1986.

Morehouse, Ellen R. "Working with Alcohol — Abusing Children of Alcoholics". **Alcohol Health and Research World,** Vol. 8(4), Summer 1984, 14-19.

✓ Morehouse, Ellen R. "Working in the Schools with Children of Alcoholic Parents". Health and Social Work, 1979, 4(4), 144-162.

Morehouse, Ellen, Richards, T. and S. Seixas. "A Child's World of Fighting and Noise". **Focus on Alcohol and Drug Issues,** 1979, 2, 16.

Morehouse, Ellen and T. Richards. "An Examination of Dysfunctional Latency Age Children of Alcoholic Parents and Problems in Intervention". **Journal of Children in Contemporary Society,** 1982, 15(1), 21-23.

Murray, R. et al. "Twin and Adoption Studies: How Good is the Evidence of a Genetic Role?" In Galanter, M. (ed.) **Recent Developments in Alcoholism,** Vol. 1, Plenum Press, New York, NY, 1983.

Musello, D. "Steady Streams of Double Messages: Adult Children of Alcoholics". **Focus on Family and Chemical Dependency,** 7(4), 9, 11, 1984.

Naiditch, B. "Intervention or Enabling — Where are the Trainers?" **Focus on Alcohol and Drug Issues,** Vol. 6(2), Mar/Apr 1983, 23.

Naiditch, B. "Why Work with Children of Alcoholics?" In Robert J. Ackerman (ed.) **Growing in the Shadow,** Health Communications, Pompano Beach, FL, 1986.

Nardi, P. "Alcohol and the Family: The Impact on Children". Association from Pitzer College, Claremont, CA, 1980.

Nardi, P. "Children of Alcoholics: A Role Theoretical Perspective". **Journal of Social Psychology,** December, 1981.

Nardi, P. "The Best Little Boy in the World: He Won't Tell". **Los Angeles Times,** March 23, 1980.

Newlin, D.B., "Offspring of Alcoholics Have Enhanced Antagonistic Placebo Response". **Journal of Studies on Alcohol** 46(6):490-494, 1985.

Nicholson, S. "Preschoolers for Chemically Dependent Families". **Focus on Alcohol and Drug Issues,** 6(4), 16-17, 1984.

Noll, R. "Young Male Offspring of Alcoholic Fathers: Early Developmental and Cognitive Differences from the MSU Vulnerability Study". **Dissertation Abstracts International,** 44(03), 922-B, 1983.

Noll, R. and R. Zucker. "Developmental Findings from an Alcoholic Vulnerability Study: The Preschool Years". Paper presented Annual Convention American Psychological Association, 1983.

Noonan, D. L. "Sex-role Conflict and Drinking Behavior in Children of Alcoholic Parents". Dissertation Abstracts International, 1981, 42, 1-B, 385.

Nylander, I. "Children of Alcoholic Fathers". **Acta Paediatrica**, 1960, 49(1), 1-134.

Nylander, I. "Children of Alcoholics Fathers". **Quarterly Journal of Studies on Alcohol,** 1963, 24, 170-172.

Nylander, I. "A Comparison Between Children of Alcoholic Fathers from Excellent Versus Poor Social Conditions". **Acta Paediatrica Scandinavica,** 71, 5, 809-813, 1982.

Obuchowska, I. "Emotional Contact with the Mother as a Social Compensatory Factor in Children of Alcoholics". **International Mental Health Research Newsletter,** 16(4), 2:4, 1974.

O'Connell, T. "The Alcoholic Family Portrait: Kids Drawings Reveal Pain, Inadequacy". U.S. **Journal of Drug and Alcohol Dependence,** Vol. 8(1), Jan 1984.

O'Gorman, P. "Self-Concept, Locus of Control, and Perception of Father in Adolescents from Homes with and without Severe Drinking Problems". Unpublished Doctoral Dissertation, Fordham University, New York, 1975.

O'Gorman, P. and R. Ross. "Children of Alcoholics in the Juvenile Justice System". **Alcohol Health and Research World,** Vol. 8(4), Summer 1984, 43-45.

O'Gorman, P. "Children of Alcoholic Parents: Prevention Issues". Paper presented at the NIAAA Symposium on Services to Children of Alcoholics, 1979.

O'Gorman P. "Public Policy and the Child of the Alcoholic". **Journal of Children in Contemporary Society,** 1982, 15(1), 35-41.

Olegard, R. et al. "Effects on the Child of Alcoholic Abuse During Pregnancy". **Acta Paediatrica Scandinavica** 275 (Suppl.), 112-121, 1979.

Olson, C. "Topical Storm: Fetal Alcohol Syndrome". **Human Ecology Forum,** Winter 1978, 9(3), 7-8.

Orme, T. and J. Rimmer. "Alcoholism and Child Abuse: A Review". **Journalism of Studies on Alcohol,** 42(3), 273-287, 1981.

Osterberg, I. "Children of Alcoholic Parents". **Nordisk Psykologi,** 1980, 32(2), 163-164.

Owen, S. et al. "Bottle-Up Children: A Group Treatment Approach for Children of Alcoholics". **Group,** 9, 3, 31-42, 1985.

Parnitzke, K.H. and O. Prussing. "Children of Alcoholic Parents". **Psychological Abstracts,** 1966, 40, 647.

Partanen, J. et al. "Inheritance of Drinking Behavior: A Study on Intelligence, Personality and Use of Alcohol in Adult Twins". Finnish Foundation for Alcohol Studies, Pub. 14, 1966.

Penick, E. et al. "Differentiation of Alcoholics by Family History". **Journal of Studies on Alcohol,** 1978, 39, 1944-48.

Perrin, T. "CoA's Dilemma: Non-existent Parents". **Focus on Family and Chemical Dependency,** Vol. 6(6), Nov/Dec 1983.

Perrin, T. "Parenting". **Alcoholism: The National Magazine,** 5(2), 23, 1984.

Pilat, J. and J. Jones. "Screening Test and Treatment Program for Children in Alcoholic Families". Paper presented at the 30th Forum of the National Council on Alcoholism, 1982.

Pilat, J. and J. Jones. "Identification of Children of Alcoholics: Two Empirical Studies". **Alcohol Health and Research World,** 1984/85, 9, 2, 26-33.

Powell, D. and B. Powell. "Alcohol and Family Violence". **Human Ecology Forum,** 1979, 9(3), 20.

Prewett, M. et al. "Attribution of Causality by Children with Alcoholic Parents". **International Journal of the Addictions,** 1981, 16(2), 367-370.

✓Priest, K. "Adolescent's Response to Parents' Alcoholism". **Social Casework,** 66(9), 533-539, 1985.

Prugh, T., "FAS Among Native Americans: Detection and Prevention". **Alcohol Health and Research World,** 10(1):36-37, 1985.

Quellette, E. et al. "Adverse Effects on Offspring of Maternal Alcohol Abuse During Pregnancy". **New England Journal of Medicine,** 297, 528-530, 1977.

Quelette, E.M. "Fetal Alcohol Syndrome". **Developmental Handicaps: Prevention and Treatment II.** Silver Springs, MD.

Quellete, E.M.; Rosett, H.L.; Rosman, N.P.; and Weiner, L. "Adverse Effects on Offspring of Maternal Alcohol Abuse During Pregnancy". **New England Journal of Medicine** 297:528-530, 1977.

Randall, C. and E. Riley. "Alcohol, Pregnancy, Babies: An Up-Date on the Latest Research — FAS/FAE". **Focus on Family and Chemical Dependency,** Vol. 7(4), July/ Aug 1984.

✓Reilly, P. "Counseling Children of Alcoholics". Paper presented at the National Council on Alcoholism Annual Forum, 1981.

"Research on Children of Alcoholics: Expanding the Knowledge". **Alcohol Health and Research World,** Vol. 8(4), Summer 1984, 6-13.

Richards, T. M. "Interventions with Adult CoAs in the Workplace". ALAMACAN, 15(9), 24-26, 1985.

Richards, T. M. "Working with Children of an Alcoholic Mother". **Alcohol and Research World,** Spring 1979.

Richards, T. M. "Splitting as a Defense Mechanism in Children of Alcoholic Parents". **Currents in Alcoholism,** 1979, 7, 239-44.

Richards, T. M., Morehouse, E., Seixas, J. and J. Kern. "Psychosocial Assessment and Intervention with Children of Alcoholic Parents". Presented at 12th Annual National Association of Social Workers, 1980.

Richards, T. M. "Alcohol Education for Young Children of Alcoholic Parents". Addictions, 1977, 5, 18-21.

Rimmer, J. "The Children of Alcoholics: An Exploratory Study". **Children and Youth Services Review,** 4, 4, 365, 1982.

Riveria-Lopez, H. "Family Ties Disruption: An Exploratory Study to Examine Alcohol Abuse Among Latino Males". **Dissertation Abstracts International,** 45(10): 3323B, 1985.

Robins, L. et al. "Father's Alcoholism and Children's Outcomes". Currents in Alcoholism, 1978, 1-V, 313-327.

Robinson, G. "Children of Alcoholics". **Social Casework,** 64, 3, 178, 1983.

Rodriguez-Andrew, S. "Los Ninos: Intervention Efforts with Mexican-American Families". **Focus on Family and Chemical Dependency,** Vol. 7(2), Mar/Apr 1984.

Rogan, A. "Issues in the Early Indentification, Assessment, and Management of Children with Fetal Alcohol Effects". **Alcohol Health and Research World,** 10(1), 66-67, 1985.

Ros, A. "The Adult Adjustment of Children of Alcoholic Parents Raised in Foster Homes". **Quarterly Journal of Studies on Alcohol,** 5, 378-393, 1944.

Roset, H. "Effects of Maternal Drinking on Child Development: An Introductory Review". **Annals of the New York Academy of Science,** 1976, 273, 115-117.

Rosner, B. "A Family Problem". **Catalyst,** 1980, 1(3), 45-47.

Rouse, B. et al. "Adolescent's Stress Levels, Coping Activities, and Father's Drinking Behavior". Proceedings of the 81st Annual Convention of the American Psychological Association, 1973, 7, 681-682.

Rydelius, P. "Children of Alcoholic Fathers: Their Social Adjustment and Their Health Status over 20 Years". **Acta Paediatrica,** 1981, 286, 7-89.

Schuckit, M. "Elevated Blood Acetaldehyde Levels in Alcoholics and Their Relatives: A Re-evaluation". **Science,** 1980, 207(21), 1383-1384.

Schall, J. "When A Parent Drinks, A Child Struggles: Here's How to Help Children Cope in Healthy Ways". **Instructor and Teacher,** 45(8), 54-57, 1986.

Scharbach, H. and C. Boucard. "Children of Alcoholic Parents: Statistical Study of the Incidence of Psychopathic and Criminological Level". **Medico-Psychologiques,** 140(7), 783-792, 1982.

Schuckit, M. "Family History and Half-Sibling Research in Alcoholism". **Annals of New York Academy of Science,** 1972, 197, 121-125.

Schuckit, M. et al. "Study of Alcoholism in Half-Siblings". **American Journal of Psychiatry,** 1972, 128(9), 1132-1136.

Sedlacek, D. "Childhood: Setting the Stage for Addiction". **Child and Youth Services,** 1983, 6(1-2), 23-24.

Seixas, J. "Coping with Alcoholic Parents". **New York Times,** May 28, 1979, 82.

Seixas, J. and M. Levitan. "Supportive Counseling Group for Adult Children of Alcoholics". **Alcoholism Treatment Quarterly,** 1984, 1, 4, 123-132.

Seixas, J. "Children from Alcohol Families". In Estes, N. and E. Heinemann, (eds.), **Alcoholism,** St. Louis, Mosby, 153-161, 1977.

Shapiro, R. "A Family Therapy Approach to Alcoholism". **Journal of Marriage and Family Counseling,** 1977, 3(4), 71-78.

Shaywitz, S. et al. "Behavior and Learning Difficulties in Children of Normal Intelligence Born to Alcoholic Mothers". **Journal of Pediatrics,** 96, 978-982, 1980.

Sher, K. and C. Descutner. "Reports of Paternal Alcoholism: Reliability Across Siblings". **Addictive Behaviors,** 11(1), 25-30, 1986.

Shirley, C. and K. Shirley. "The Process of Recovery for the Alcoholic and the Family". New York Affiliate, Inc., National Council on Alcoholism, 1981.

Shruygin, G. "Characteristics of the Mental Development of Children of Alcoholic Mothers". **Pediatriya** (Moscow), 11, 71-73, 1974.

Sierra, J. "The Minority Family with Alcoholism". Paper presented at National Council on Alcoholism Annual Forum, 1981.

Sloboda, S. "The Children of Alcoholics: A Neglected Problem". **Hospital and Community Psychiatry,** 1974, 25(9), 605-606.

✓ Smith, C. "Overview of Personality, Behavior and Parental Alcoholism". **Currents in Alcoholism,** 1978, 5, 297-299.

Snel, A. "Project Rainbow Helps Kids Right Alcohol Problems". Rockland County Times, August 21, 1980.

Steinglass, P. "Experimenting with Family Treatment Approaches to Alcoholism: 1950-1975 A Review". **Family Process,** 1976, 15, 97-123.

Steinglass, P. "Alcohol as a Member of the Family". **Human Ecology Forum,** 1978, 9(3), 9-11.

Steinglass, P. "A Life History Model of the Alcoholic Family". **Family Process,** 1980, 19, 211-226.

Steinhausen, H. et al. "Psychopathology and Mental Functions in the Offspring of Alcohol and Epileptic Mothers". **Journal of the American Academy of Child Psychiatry,** 21, 268-273, 1982.

Steinhausen, H. et al. "Psychopathology in the Offspring of Alcoholic Parents". **Journal of the American Academy of Child Psychiatry,** 23, 4. 465-471, 1984.

✓ Stevens, D. M. "Some Adjustment Characteristics of the Adolescent Children of Alcoholic Parents". Dissertation Abstracts, 1968, 29, 1-A, 156.

✓ Straussner, S. et al. "Effects of Alcoholism on the Family System." **Health and Social Work,** 1979, 4(4), 111-127.

Streissguth, A. et al. "Intelligence, Behavior, and Dysmorphogenesis in the Fetal Alcohol Syndrome: A Report on 20 Patients". **Journal of Pediatrics,** 92, 363-367, 1978.

Streissguth, A. and R. LaDue. "Psychological and Behavioral Effects in Children Prenatally Exposed to Alcohol". **Alcohol Health and Research World,** 10, 16-12, 1985.

Streissguth, A. et al. "Offspring Effects and Pregnancy Complications Related to Self-Reported Maternal Alcohol Use". **Developmental Pharmacology and Therapeutics,** 5, 21-32, 1982.

Streissguth, A. et al. "Natural History of the Fetal Alcohol Syndrome: A 10-Year Follow-Up of Eleven Patients" **Lancet,** 2, 85-91, 1985.

Stuckey, R. "Daughters of Alcoholics and the Women's Movement: A Commentary". **Focus on Family and Chemical Dependency,** 8(3), 30-31, 1985.

Swinson, R. "Sex Differences in the Inheritance of Alcoholism". In O. Kalant (ed.), **Research Advances in Alcohol and Drug Problems: Alcohol and Drug Problems in Women,** Vol. 5., Plenum Press, New York, 1980.

Tartar, R. et al. "Adolescent Sons of Alcoholics: Neuropsychological and Personality Characteristics". **Alcoholism: Clinical and Experimental Research,** 8(2), 216-222, 1984.

Tec, N. "Parent-Child Drug Abuse: Generation Continuity or Adolescent Deviance?" **Adolescence,** 1974, 9(35), 351-364.

"The Alcoholic Family at Home". **Archives of General Psychiatry,** 1981, 38(3), 578-584.

"The Alcoholic Family in the Interaction Laboratory". **Journal of Nervous and Mental Disease,** 1979, 428-436.

Tippman, J. "The Forgotten Victims: Children of Alcoholics". Master of Social Work Thesis, State Univeristy of New York, Stonebrook, 1980.

Trama, J.A. "Comparison of the Impact of An Alcohol Education Program with Al-Anon on Knowledge and Attitudes About Alcoholism and Perceptions of the Family Environment". Ohio State University, Columbus, OH, Dissertation Abstracts International 45(8):2668A, 1985.

Triplett, J. and S. Arneson. "Children of Alcoholic Parents: A Neglected Issue". **Journal of School Health,** 1978, 48, 596-599.

Utne, H. et al. "Alcohol Elimination Rates with and without Alcoholic Parents". **Journal of Studies on Alcohol,** 1977, 38(7), 1219-1223.

✓Vargas, J. et al. "Emotional and Developmental Aspects of Children of Alcoholic Parents". **Gaceta Neuro-Psiquiatrica,** 1978, 2(10), 3145.

Virkkunen, M. "Incest Offenses and Alcoholism". **Medicine, Science and Law,** 1974, 14, 224-228.

Vitez, M. et al. "A Semiquantitative Score System for Epidemiologic Studies of Fetal Alcohol Syndrome". **American Journal of Epidemiology** 119(3):301-308, 1984.

Waite, B. and M. Ludwig. "A Growing Concern: How to Provide Services for Children from Alcoholic Families". Evaluation Technologies Inc. Available from: Superintendent of Documents, US Government Printing Office, Washington, DC 20402.

Wanck, B. "Treatment of Adult Children of Alcoholics". **Carrier Foundation Letter,** #109, September, 1985.

Wald, P. "Project Rainbow Brings Hope to Troubled Children". **Rockland Review,** August 8, 1979.

Warner, R. and H. Rosett. "Effects of Drinking on Offspring". **Journal of Studies on Alcohol,** 1975, 36, 1395-1420.

Watters, T. and W. Theimer. "Children of Alcoholics — A Critical Review of Some Literature". **Contemporary Drug Problems,** 1978, 7(2), 195-201.

Wegscheider, S. "Co-dependency: The Therapeutic Void". **Focus on Family and Chemical Dependency,** Vol. 6(6) Nov/Dec 1983.

Wegscheider, S. "From Reconstruction to Restoration". **Focus on Family and Chemical Dependency,** Vol. 6(5). Sept/Oct 1983.

Wegscheider, S. "Children of Alcoholics Caught in Family Trap". **Focus on Alcohol and Drug Issues,** May/June 1979, 2,8.

Wegsheider, S. "From the Family Trap to Family Freedom". **Alcoholism,** 1981, 1(3), 36-39.

Weit, W. "Counseling Youth Whose Parents are Alcoholic: A Means to an End as Well as an End in Itself". **Journal of Alcohol Education,** 1970, 16(1), 13-19.

Werner, E. "Resilient Offspring of Alcoholics: A Longitudinal Study from Birth to Age 18". **Journal of Studies on Alcohol,** 47(1), 34-40, 1986.

Wert, R. "Effects of Parental Alcoholism and Personal Level of Alcohol Consumption on Abstract Reasoning Performance". **Dissertation Abstracts International,** 46(7), 2469B-2470B, 1986.

Whitfield, C. "Co-Alcoholism: Recognizing a Treatable Illness". **Family & Community Health,** Vol. 7, Summer 1984.

Whitfield, C. "Children of Alcoholics: Treatment Issues". **Maryland State Medical Journal,** 1980, 29(6), 86-91.

Whitlock, F. "Alcoholism: A Genetic Disorder?". **Australian and New Zealand Journal of Psychiatry,** 1975, 9, 3-7.

Williams, C. "Differences in Child Care Practices Among Families with Alcoholic Fathers, Alcoholic Mothers, and Two Alcoholic Parents". **Dissertation Abstracts International,** 44(01), 299-A, 1983.

Williams, K. "Children of Alcoholic Parents: Intervention Issues". Paper presented at NIAAA Symposium on Services to Children of Alcoholics, 1979.

Wilson C. et al. "An Exploratory Study of the Relationship Between Child Abuse Neglect and Alcohol/Drug Abuse". Tennessee Department of Human and Social Services, Alcohol and Drug Section, Memphis State University, College of Education, June 1977.

Wilson, C. and J. Oxford. "Children of Alcoholics". **Journal of Studies on Alcohol,** 1978, 39(1), 121-140.

Wilson, C. and J. Oxford. "Children of Alcoholics: A Preliminary Report on the Literature". **International Journal of Rehabilitation Research,** 1980, 3(1), 94-96.

Wilson, J.B. "Family Communication, Interpersonal Influence and Teenage Alcohol Consumption", Washington University, St. Louis, MO, **Dissertation Abstracts International,** 46(3):800A, 1985.

Woititz, J. "Adult Children of Alcoholics". Paper presented at National Council on Alcoholism Annual Forum, 1981.

Woititz, J. "Common Characteristics of Adult Children of Alcoholics". In Robert J. Ackerman (ed) **Growing in the Shadow,** Health Communications, Pompano Beach, FL, 1986.

Wolin, S. and L. Bennett. "Heritage Continuity Among the Children of Alcoholics". In E. Gottheil et al. **Etiologic Aspects of Alcohol and Drug Abuse,** Charles C. Thomas, Springfield, IL, 1983.

Wolin, S. et al. "Disrupted Family Rituals" **Journal of Studies on Alcohol,** 1980, 41(3), 199-213.

Wolin, S. et al. "Family Rituals and the Recurrence of Alcoholism over Generations". **American Journal of Psychiatry,** 1979, 136(4B), 589-593.

Worden, M. "Living with What You Know, But are Forced to Deny". **The U.S. Journal of Drug and Alcohol Dependence,** Vol. 8(8), Aug 1984, 13.

Worden, M. "Developmental Model Key to Understanding". **The U.S. Journal of Drug and Alcohol Dependence,** Vol. 8(8), Aug 1984, p. 13.

Worden, M. "The Children of Alcoholics Movement: Honeymoon Spirit, Optimism Prevail Despite Unclear Future". **The U.S. Journal of Drug and Alcohol Dependence,** Vol. 8(10), Oct 1984, 12-13.

Worden, M. "The Children of Alcoholics Movement: Early Frontiers". **The U. S. Journal of Drug and Alcohol Dependence,** Vol. 8(9), Sept 1984, 12-13.

Worden, M. "Children of Alcoholics: Growing Up in Dysfunctional Families". **Focus on Family and Chemical Dependency,** Vol. 7(4), July/Aug 1984.

"Young Children of Alcoholics Target of Prevention Program". Children of Alcoholics, A Special Report National Institute on Alcohol Abuse and Alcoholism, January, 1984.

(44) BIBLIOGRAPHY

PAMPHLETS AND BOOKLETS

Source: Al-Anon/Alateen Family Group
Headquarters, Inc.
P.O. Box 862
Midtown Station
New York, NY 10018-0862

Titles: Adult Children of Alcoholics
Al-Anon is for Adult Children of Alcoholics
Al-Anon Sharings from Adult Children
of Alcoholics
Al-Anon Speaks Out:
A Community Resource
Did you Grow Up with a Problem Drinker?
Alateen: Hope for Children of Alcoholics
Facts about Alateen
Guide for the Family of an Alcoholic
For Teenagers with an Alcoholic Parent
How Can I Help My Children?
If Your Parents Drink Too Much
Living With an Alcoholic: With the Help
of Al-Anon
Process of Recovery: Al-Anon &
the Adult Child
So You Love an Alcoholic
The Process of Recovery: Al-Anon and the
Adult Child
Twelve Steps and Twelve Traditions
for Alateen
What Do You Do About the Alcoholic's
Drinking?
What's "Drunk", Mama?
Youth and the Alcoholic Parent

Source: Alcoholics Anonymous World Services, Inc.
P.O. Box 459
Grand Central Station
New York, NY 10163-1100

Title: AA—44 Questions
Is There an Alcoholic in Your Life?

Source: Addiction Research Foundation Department
c/o Marketing Services
33 Russell Street
Toronto, Ontario,
Canada M55 2S1

Title: Alcoholism and The Family
Alcoholism — A Merry-Go-Round
  Named Denial

Source: Children of Alcoholics
  Foundations, Inc.
200 Park Ave., 31st Floor
New York, NY 10166

Title: Children of Alcoholics: A Report to
  Hugh L. Carey, Governor,
State of New York, New York.
Children of Alcoholics
  Foundation, 1982.

Children of Alcoholics: A Review of the
  Literature.
New York: Children of Alcoholics Foun-
  dation, 1985.

Report of the Conference on Research Needs
  and Opportunities for Children of
Alcoholics.
New York: Children of Alcoholics
  Foundation, 1984.

Source: CompCare Publications
2415 Annapolis Lane
Minneapolis, MN 55441

Titles: The Family Enabler

Source: Hazelden Educational Materials Press
Pleasant Valley Road
Box 176
Center City, MN 55012-0176

Titles: Alcohol, A Family Affair
Alcoholism, A Family Illness (Smithers
    Foundation)
Alcoholism, A Family Illness (Betty Reddy)
Brown Bottle, A Fable for Children of All
Ages (P. Jones), 1983, 40.
Children of Alcoholics, Pickens
Fetal Alcohol Syndrome
Guide for the Family of the Alcoholic
Hope for Young People with Alcoholic
    Parents
I Should Be Happy . . . Why Do I Hurt?
Learn About Children of Alcoholics
My House is Different
New Pamphlet Series for Adult Children
    (Larsen)
For Troubled Teens with Problem Parents
When Daddy's a Drunk . . . What to Tell Kids

Source: Thomas W. Perrin, Inc.
Perrin & Treggett
P.O. Box 190, 5 Glen Rd.
Rutherford, N.J. 07070

Titles: Care & Management of Flashbacks (Perrin)
Child Abuse and Alcoholism, (L. Russell)
Dimensions of Surrogate Parent
    Relationships,

Griefwork & the Adult Children of Alcoholic Families, (D. Frye)

The Growing Child with Fetal Alcohol Syndrome

Forgiving Our Parents, (Perrin)

I Am An Adult Who Grew Up In An Alcoholic Family, (Perrin)

Living With Chronic Depression, (Perrin)

Parenting, (Perrin)

Psychotherapy with Adult Children of Alcoholics: A Structured Group Model, (Perrin)

Treatment Priorities for Alcoholics and Their Families, (Perrin)

Source: Public Affairs Pamphlets
381 Park Avenue South
New York, NY 10016

Titles: You and Your Alcoholic Parent
by Edith Lynn Nornik

Source: National Clearinghouse for
Alcohol Information
P.O. Box 2345
Rockville, MD. 20852

Titles: National Institute on Alcohol Abuse and Alcoholism. A Growing Concern: How to Provide Services for Children from Alcoholic Families.

National Institute on Alcohol Abuse and Alcoholism. Services for Children of Alcoholics. Research Monograph No. 4. DHHS Pub. No. (ADM) 81-1007. Preventing Alcohol Problems Through a Student Assistance Program, G. Snyder.

Source: National Council on Alcoholism
Michigan Division
2875 Northwind, Suite 225
East Lansing, MI 48823

Title: Catalyst. Issue features articles on children of
alcoholics.

Source: Rutgers Center for Alcohol Studies
Publication Division
New Brunswick, NJ 08903

Titles: Adjustment of the Family to the Crisis of
Alcoholism, by Joan K. Jackson
Alcohol-Related Acts of Violence: Who Was
Drinking and Where the Acts Occurred by
L. W. Gerson
The Alcoholic's Spouse, Children and Family
Interaction: Substantive Findings and
Methodological Issues by T. Jacobs,
A. Favorini, S.S. Meisel and M. Anderson
Alcoholism and Child Abuse: A Review by
T.C. Orme and J. Rimmer
Children of Alcoholics, A Report of a Preli-
minary Study and Comments on the Litera-
ture by C. Wilson and J. Orford
Disrupted Family Rituals: A Factor in the
Intergenerational Transmission of Alco-
holism by S.J. Wolin, L. Bennett, D.
Noonan and M. Teitelbaum
The Effects of Drinking on Offspring: A His-
torical Survey of the American and British
Literature by R. Warner and H. Rosett
Family Therapy with the Families of Recover-
ing Alcoholics by D. Meeks and C. Kelly

Source: Health Communications, Inc.
1721 Blount Rd.
Pompano Beach, FL 33069

Titles: Adult Children of Alcoholics: Common Char-
acteristics by J. G. Woititz
Children of Alcoholics: Understanding and
Helping by C. Deutsch
Co-Dependency and Family Rules A Paradox-
ical Dependency by R. Subby and J. Friel
Co-Dependency and the Search for Identity by
R. Subby, J. Friel and L. Friel
Chronic Shock: And Adult Children of Alco-
holics by W. Kritsberg
Guidelines for Support Groups: Adult Children
of Alcoholics and Others Who Identify
by J.G. Woititz
Reflections on Our Childhood: 3 Stories
by J. Greenleaf
Primer on Adult Children of Alcoholics
by T. L. Cermak
Chemical Dependency: A Systems Illness
by S. Wegscheider
Alcoholism and Incest in the Family
by C. Barnard

Source: National Association for Children of
Alcoholics
31706 Coast Highway
Suite 201
South Laguna, CA. 92677

Titles: Children of Alcoholics: Meeting the Needs of
the Young CoA in the School Setting by
E. Morehouse and C. Scola

Children of Alcoholics: Who They Are, What
They Experience, How They Recover
by H. Gravitz

Source: C.O.A. Books
P.O. Box 17994
Salem, OR 97305

Title: Children of Alcoholics in Play Therapy by
Mary L. Hammond

(52) BIBLIOGRAPHY

AUDIOVISUALS
FILMS

Alcoholism, A Family Problem
(13 minutes), 1978
This film presents a dramatization of three stages of alcoholism as it affects family members. It explores the feelings and behaviors typical of each stage.
Available from:
Health Sciences Consortium
200 Eastone Drive
Suite 213
Chapel Hill, NC

Alcoholism and the Family
(42 minutes), 1977
This program points out the effect of alcoholism on the family before and after sobriety.
Available from:
FMS Productions, Inc.
1777 North Vine Street
Los Angeles, CA 90028

All Alone Together
(43 minutes), 1983
Produced by a recovering alcoholic for WCCO-TV in Minneapolis, this film is the true story of a suburban family nearly destroyed by alcohol and other drugs. Two alcoholic parents and three children with drug problems reenact their own experiences of near-disintegration, painful growth and recovery.
Available from:
CompCare Publications
2415 Annapolis Lane
Minneapolis, MN

All Bottled Up
(29 minutes), 1975
This film highlights the child's perspective of alcoholic parents.
Available from:
> AIMS Media Inc.
> 626 Hustin Avenue
> Glendale, CA 91201

Another Chance
(30 minutes)
In this film, Sharon Wegscheider presents a storyline based on Mary Lee, from a co-dependent home, who grew up in a tense atmosphere of fear, guilt, etc. Sharon guides Mary Lee in an exploration of her feelings relating to situations not only in her own past, but also of other family members.
Available from:
> Onsite Training and Consulting, Inc.
> 2820 W. Main St.
> Rapid City, SD 57702

Bitter Wind
This film presents the story of a Navajo family and the attempts of a son to reunite his alcoholic family.
Available from:
> Department of Audio-Visual Communications
> Brigham Young Univerity
> Provo, UT 84601

Children of Alcohol
(18 minutes, color)
Describes a therapeutic camping trip for children from alcoholic homes. General audiences.
Available from:
> Kinetic Films, Inc.
> 255 Delaware Ave
> Buffalo, NY 14202

Children of Denial
(28 minutes)
This film features Claudia Black speaking about youngsters, adolescents, and adults as children of alcoholics. Three basic tenets rule the lives of these children — don't talk — don't trust — don't feel.
Available from:
    A.C.T.
    P.O. Box 8536
    Newport Beach, CA 92660

Choicemaking
(30 minutes), 1984
Sharon Wegscheider-Cruse is featured in this film for Co-dependents, Adult Children and Spirituality Seekers. Recovery is a challenge, full of many more choices than just getting well. This film offers a bridge between therapy and continuing recovery at home. It helps the dependent family members make full use of recovery as the ultimate opportunity for growth and spiritual fulfillment.
Available from:
    Onsite Training
    2820 W. Main St.
    Rapid City, SD 57702

Drinking Parents
(10 minutes)
Through conversations with a recovered alcoholic mother and her teenaged daughter, the feelings and frustrations of their situation are discussed from both viewpoints. The primary objective of this film is to emphasize that young people with alcoholic parents can get help from community resources, and not remain isolated.
Available from:
    MTI Teleprograms, Inc.
    4825 North Scoot Street
    Suite 23
    Schiller Park, IL 60176

The Enablers
(23 minutes)
This film shows how the family and friends of an alcoholic working woman, unknowingly enable her to progress into alcoholism. The audience see the repercussions of the illness in the lives of people around the alcoholic.
Available from:
   Johnson Institute
   510 First Ave., N.
   Minneapolis, MN 55403

Everyone A Winner
(4 minutes)
Breakfast time conflict in a family is resolved with anger, door-slamming and retreat. Alone, the wife turns to two comforts — a drink and a phone call to mother. (A short open-ended film intended to trigger discussion.)
Available from:
   National Publications
   P.O. Box 4116
   Omaha, NB 68104

Families of Alcoholics
(15 minutes), 1983.
A segment of ABC's report by Geraldo Rivera. Explores the despair, hopes, and fears of family members. High school and above.
Available from:
   MTI Teleprograms, Inc.
   3710 Commercial Avenue
   Northbrook, IL 60060
   (800)323-5343

Family Business
(30 minutes)
This film describes the behavior patterns of adult children of alcoholics. It is shown how therapists and self-help groups can help ACA's break old patterns, learn new behaviors, and improve their self-concept.

Available from:
> Ergo Media
> 1999 N. Sycamore St.
> Los Angeles, CA 90068.

Family Matters
(30 minutes, color)
A Dick Young Production for Hazelden. Five different families. Each from different life experiences. Each touched by the tragedy of addiction. Family members of all ages will see the problems addiction can trigger; the family can survive and thrive.
Available from:
> Hazelden Press
> Pleasant Valley Road
> Center City, MN 55012-0176

A Family Talks About Alcohol ✓
(30 minutes), 1983.
This film dramatizes the problems experienced by a family as a result of one alcoholic member. Junior and senior high.
Available from:
> Perennial Education, Inc.
> 930 Pitner Avenue
> Evanston, IL 60202
> (800)323-9084

The Family Trap
(30 minutes)
Presented by Sharon Wegscheider, this film offers the first complete picture of the pressures which contribute to the family illness, and the hope and help there is for family members to achieve recovery through intervention, identification and counseling.
Available from:
> Onsite Training
> 2820 W. Main St.
> Rapid City, SD 57702

Francesca Baby
(45 minutes)
Two daughters, ages 16 and 10, attempt to cope with their mother's alcoholism. This film portrays the effects on the daughters and the beginnings of recovery through Alateen. This film is appropriate for adolescents and adult audiences.
Available from:
> Walt Disney Studios
> Burbank, CA

The Game
(28 minutes), 1977
This film focuses on two families (one affluent, one blue collar) who are having difficulties with alcohol. The affluent alcoholic is an active drinker who realizes he needs help with his drinking problem, while the blue collar man is a recovering alcoholic who finds returning to his family a rewarding experience.
Available from:
> University of Connecticut
> Media and the Arts for Social Science
> U-Box 127
> Storrs, CT 06268

Getting Them Sober
(30 minutes)
A group of counselors and spouses of alcoholics discuss the impediments to the recovery of the families of alcoholics. Topics of discussion include: (1) fear, guilt and anger (2) denial (3) enabling (4) counselor reactions and (5)Al-Anon.
Available from:
> Maryland Publishing Co.
> P.O. Box 19910
> Baltimore, MD 21211

Hope for the Children
(28 minutes, color)
Problems faced by 5 to 12-year-old children of alcoholics, as well as vignettes from therapy groups. Designed to train and

motivate adults to intervene.
Available from:
> Health Communications
> 1721 Blount Rd.
> Pompano Beach, FL 33069

If You Loved Me
(54 minutes)
Chronicles the almost-classic deterioration of a family because of alcoholism. The arguing, the tears, the frustrations, and the denial. Finally the wife accepts a friend's advice to go to a meeting of Al-Anon.
Available from:
> Gerald T. Rogers Productions
> 5225 Old Orchard Road
> Suite 23
> Skokie, IL 60077

The Intervention
(28 minutes)
The family portrayed in **The Enablers** seeks information about alcoholism. They learn that their action can motivate the alcoholic wife and mother to get help, as well as initiate a recovery process for the other family members.
Available from:
> Johnson Institute
> 510 First Ave., N.
> Minneapolis, MN 55403

Intervention and Recovery
(30 minutes), 1982
This film is intended to introduce the concept of intervention to family, friends, and employers who want to help the alcoholic or drug addicted person.
Available from:
> FMS Productions, Inc.
> 1777 North Vine Street
> Los Angeles, CA 90028

Lots of Kids Like Us
(28 minutes, color)
A small boy and his sister try to cope with their father's alcoholism. Gives children the messages: "You are not alone," and "It's not your fault."
Available from:
    Gerald T. Rogers Productions, Inc.
    5225 Old Orchard RR., Suite 23
    Skokie, IL 60077
    (312) 967-8080

Living with an Alcoholic Parent
(30 minutes)
Maternal alcohol consumption and the effects on the fetus.
Available from:
    Fetal Alcohol Education Program
    7 Kent St.
    Brookline, MA 02146

My Father's Son
(33 minutes, color)
This new film for adolescents and families follows the sixteen-year old son of an alcoholic who is trying to lead a normal life amid the chaos of a dysfunctioning family. It is especially effective for children of alcoholics.
Available from:
    Gerald T. Rogers Productions
    5225 Old Orchard Road, Suite 23
    Skokie, IL 60077
    (312)967-8080

Pregnancy on the Rocks:
The Fetal Alcohol Syndrome
(26 minutes, color)
This film presents a searing examination of the effects of alcohol on babies whose mothers drank while pregnant. Interviews with families and children lend startling, often poig-

nant insight into this affliction.
Available from:
    Hazelden Press
    Pleasant Valley Road
    Box 176
    Center City, MN 55012-0176

One for My Baby
(27 minutes), 1982
This film presents information about fetal alcohol syndrome
(FAS). Discussed are the symptoms of FAS as well as the
relative risks to the unborn, when women drink during pregnancy. Two couples who have FAS children — one natural
born, one adopted — are interviewed, and describe their feelings about the syndrome as the camera focuses on the
children.
Available from:
    WHA-TV Distribution Department
    821 University Avenue
    Madison, WI 53706

Romance to Recovery
(38 minutes)
The story of Dick and Jane, Richie and Janie, in their predict-
able but preventable alcoholic/co-alcoholic relationship. It
follows them through cover up, manipulation, medical complications, child abuse, remorse, separation, revenge, and
reunion. It focuses on the recovery of both the alcoholic and
the co-alcoholic.
Available from:
    FMS Productions, Inc.
    1777 North Vine Street
    Los Angeles, CA 90028

The Secret Love of Sandra Blain
(28 minutes), 1970
This film presents a step-by-step dramatization of the pro-
gression into alcoholism of a wife and mother, showing how

her unrecognized illness affects her family, friends, physician and herself.
Available from:
> Brigham Young University
> Media Marketing W-STAD
> Provo, UT 84602

She Drinks A Little
(31 minutes), 1981
Teenager Cindy Stott has an alcoholic mother whose drinking is destroying both their lives. With the help of a male classmate with a similar problem, Cindy discovers Alateen and learns how to deal with her mother.
Available from:
> Learning Corporation of America
> 1350 Avenue of the Americas
> New York, NY 10019

Soft is the Heart of a Child
(30 minutes), 1980
This film depicts through drama, the effects of alcoholism on the family, especially the children. The focus is on the trauma of the children and the need for professionals to respond. This film is particularly effective with school personnel and for sensitizing concerned adults.
Available from:
> Gerald T. Rogers Productions
> 5225 Old Orchard Road
> Suite 6
> Skokie, IL 60077

A Story About Feelings
(10 minutes, color)
This film uses cartoons to teach five to eight-year-old children how drinking, using drugs, and smoking are unwise choices for changing feelings. Family services, children's organizations, and prevention agencies can use this film to help chil-

dren understand and express their feelings.
Available from:
> Hazelden Press
> Pleasant Valley Rd.
> Center City, MN 55012-017

The Struggle for Intimacy
1985
Dr. Janet Woititz discusses in this film the need for health relationships and how children of alcoholics struggle to achieve them. Ways to achieve intimacy are discussed by Dr. Woititz.
Available from:
> Health Communications, Inc.
> 1721 Blount Road
> Pompano Beach, FL 33069

Suffer the Children
Delineates the problems faced by children growing up in an alcoholic home. Interviews several children as well as a recently sober mother plus Dr. Claudia Black, a therapist for children of alcoholic parents. Adults.
Available from:
> Carousel Film and Video
> 241 East 34th Street, Room 304
> New York, NY 10016
> (212)683-1660

The Summer We Moved to Elm Street
(30 minutes), 1968
In this film, the family of an alcoholic is shown through the eyes of a nine-year-old daughter.
Available from:
> McGraw-Hill Films
> 330 West 42nd Street
> New York, NY 10036

(64) BIBLIOGRAPHY

VIDEOCASSETTES

Adult Children of Alcoholics
(35 minutes) 1985
Dr. Janet Woititz is featured in this tape discussing her work and insights into the problems confronting adult children of alcoholics. Characteristics and explanations for the behaviors of many adult children of alcoholics are explored. This tape is valuable for all adult children of alcoholics and for those working with adult children.
Available from:
    Alcoholism Counselors
    Continuing Education Services
    3901 Meadows Drive, B-1
    Indianapolis, IN 46205

Adult Children of Alcoholics:
Choices for Growth
(55 minutes) 1985
This tape features Dr. Robert Ackerman before a live audience discussing and presenting information about adult children of alcoholics and how and why they are affected differently. During the presentation his sense of humor, knowledge and empathy add greatly to the understanding of adult children of alcoholics by examining their childhood, where they are now, and what choices are available to them for future growth. Highly recommended for adult children of alcoholics and those working with them.
Available from:
    Addiction Research & Consulting Services
    116 Cambridge Street
    Indiana, PA 15701

Alcohol and the Family: The Breaking Point
(29 minutes)
This video portrays the effects of alcoholism on the family.
Available from:
Aims Media
6901 Woodley Avenue
Van Nuys, CA 91406-9980

Alcoholism in the Family
(58 minutes)
Patrick Gannon, Ph.D., 1980. Clinical Training Program:
Part of an NIAAA funded program at the California School
of Professional Psychology, Berkeley, CA. Identifies hidden
alcoholic parents in families with adolescents referred for
drug abuse.
Available from:
Health Media Services
367 Liberty St.
San Francisco, CA 94114

A Child's View
(36 minutes) 1987
Dr. Claudia Black presents aa explanation of alcohol and
drug abuse for children using pictures.
Available from:
M.A.C.
1850 High Street
Denver, CO 80218

Children of Alcohol
(18 minutes) 1984
Children of alcoholic parents discuss their feelings and attitudes on the subject of alcohol abuse. The children range in
age from 8 to 15 years. This film gives hope to other children
of alcoholics who may feel isolated, perhaps teaching them to

ask for help rather than keep their parent's alcoholism a secret.
Available from:
> Kinetic Film Enterprises, Ltd
> 255 Delaware Ave., Suite 340
> Buffalo, NY 14202

Children of Alcoholics
(38 minutes), 1982
Designed for use with therapists, counselors and other professionals, this videocassette features Dr. Robert Ackerman discussing the special treatment needs for working with children of alcoholics and their families.
Available from:
> Addiction Research and Consulting Services
> 116 Cambridge Street
> Indiana, PA 15701

Children of Alcoholics
(30 minutes)
Sharon Wegsheider explores the development of dysfunctional behavior patterns that become normal survival coping for children of alcoholics. In understanding these roles, we are better equipped to help children choose to change. Provides understanding, compassion, and support.
Available from:
> Onsite Training and Consulting, Inc.
> 2820 W. Main Street
> Rapid City, SD 57702

Co-Dependency
(30 minutes)
Sharon Wegscheider discusses co-dependency as a primary disease and one within every member of an alcoholic family. It is what happens to family members when they try to adapt to a sick family system that seeks to protect and enable the

alcoholic. Each family member enters into this collusion in his or her own way.
Available from:
Onsite Training and Consulting, Inc.
2820 W. Main Street
Rapid City, SD 57702

Family Aftercare and Recovery
(30 minutes)
People going home after treatment want things to be different without change. In this presentation, Sharon Wegscheider explains why and how to a group of people preparing to go back to their families. She outlines the requirements for care after treatment and full recovery for the family in every respect.
Available from:
Onsite Training and Consulting, Inc.
2820 W. Main Street
Rapid City, SD 57702

Family Business
(30 minutes)
This film describes the behavior patterns of adult children of alcoholics (ACoAs). These coping mechanisms are learned early through observation of the alcoholic parent and the co-dependent. These behaviors include denial, distortion of the truth, suppression of emotions, depression, people-pleasing, and rescuing. It is shown how therapists and self-help groups can help ACA's break old patterns, learn new behaviors and improve their self-concept.
Available from:
Ergo Media
1999 N. Sycamore Street
Los Angeles, CA 90068

Open Secrets
(30 minutes)
A family caught up in a chain of events that results in tragedy

(a drunk driving fatality) is portrayed. The family's failure to confront the issues of drug and alcohol use within their own home is examined.
Available from:
> MTI Teleprograms,Inc.
> 108 Wilmot Road
> Deerfield, IL 60015

Recovery
(45 minutes) 1987
This video features Claudia Black and is designed for Adult Children of Alcoholics who are ready to begin recovery.
Available from:
> M.A.C.
> 1850 High Street
> Denver, CO 80218

Roles
(42 minutes) 1987
Four roles of children of alcoholics called the Responsible One, the Adjuster, the Placater and the Acting Out One are presented and discussed by Dr. Claudia Black.
Available from:
> M.A.C.
> 1850 High Street
> Denver, CO 80218

Sculpturing
(30 minutes)
Sharon Wegscheider uses sculpturing, a technique in which family members are physically placed in positions symbolizing their feelings — a vivid demonstration showing how chemical dependency fragments and destroys the unity of the family system.
Available from:
> Onsite Training and Consulting Inc.
> 2820 W. Main St.
> Rapid City, SD 57702

Substance Abuse:
Fetal Alcohol Syndrome, Part I
(57 mins)
Available from:
    National Center for Education
      in Maternal and Child Health
    38th and R Streets, NW
    Washington, DC 20057

That's Marilyn
(28 minutes), 1980
This is a dramatic program about the children of alcoholics
and provides an understanding of some of the sufferings of
thousands of young people in our communities. Designed for
teenage and adult audiences, this videotape will spark a sym-
pathetic discussion on these issues.
Available from:
    Aims Media, Inc.
    626 Hustin Avenue
    Glendale, CA 91201

AUDIOCASSETTES

Children of Alcoholic Parents
  by Frank G. Stone

Availability:
  Hogg Foundation Library
  Hogg Foundation for Mental Health
  P.O. Box 7998
  The University of Texas
  Austin, TX 78712

Counseling the Children of Alcoholics
  by Kathleen Michael

Availability:
  AIMS Media, Inc.
  626 Hustin Avenue
  Glendale, CA 91201

Fetal Alcohol Syndrome
  by Mary Jane Ashley
Availability:
  Addiction Research Foundation
  33 Russell Street
  Toronto, Ontario, Canada M55 2S1

Hope for Adult Children of Alcoholics, Album 13
These four cassettes give an in-depth look at some of the problems and concerns shared among children of alcoholics. The speakers bring their own personal or professional exper-

ience to their topics and provide excellent discussion material for groups of Adult Children of Alcoholics.

Fulfillment in Recovery, Ernie Larsen, Side 1.
Decisions and Choices, Elene Loecher, Side 2.
Adult Relationships, Robert Subby, Side 1.
Stages of Growth, Barbara Naiditch, Side 2.
Grief and Loss, Marty Kreuzzer, Side 1.
The Twelve Steps and ACoA, Sondra S., Side 2.
Reflections, Bob W., Side 1.
Reflections, Ellen W., Side 2.

Availability:

Hazelden
Audio-Cassette Series
Pleasant Valley Road
Box 176
Center City, MN 55012-0176

Human Development and Children of Alcoholics
by Robert J. Ackerman

Family Response to Addiction
by Robert J. Ackerman

Adult Children of Alcoholics: Growth and Choices
by Robert J. Ackerman

Adult Children of Alcoholics and Emotional Intimacy
by Robert J. Ackerman

Alcohol Abuse and Child Abuse
by Robert J. Ackerman

Availability:
Addiction Research & Consulting Services
116 Cambridge Street
Indiana, PA 15701

Co-Dependency/Children of Alcoholics
  by Sharon Wegscheider
Alcoholic Family Challenges
  by Sharon Wegscheider
Making Choices/The Hidden Illness
  by Sharon Wegscheider

Availability:
  Onsite Training and Consulting, Inc.
  2820 W. Main Street
  Rapid City, SD 57702

Parents with Alcoholism: Kids with Hope
Explores the many ways a parent's drinking problem affects
the entire family. Draws on actual case studies to present the
kinds of situations often experienced by children of alcoholics.

Availability:
  Human Relations Media
  175 Tompkins Ave.
  Pleasantville, NY 100570

Adult Children of Alcoholics
  by Janet Woititz
Alcoholic Family as Learning
  by Jael Greenleaf
Alcoholic Family Pattern
  by Rokelle Lerner
Beyond Survival
  by Cathleen Brooks
Co-Dependency: Primary Diagnosis
  by Charles Whitfield
Families and Alcoholism
  by Janet Woititz
The Hope of Recovery
  by Robert Subby
The Hurried Child Syndrome
  by Robert Subby

Intimate Relationships and Adult Children of Alcoholics
by Janet Woititz
Spirituality and Co-Dependency
by Charles Whitfield
Support Groups for Adolescent Children of Alcoholics
by Cathleen Brooks
Teen Alcoholism in Chemically Dependent Families
by Patricia O'Gorman
What About the Children
by Janet Woititz

Availability:
Alcoholism Counselors Continuing Education Services
3901 Meadows Drive, B-1
Indianapolis, IN 46205

Say Yes To Life
by Rokelle Lerner and Joseph Cruse

Availability:
Health Communications, Inc.
1721 Blount Road,
Pompano Beach, FL 33069

MISCELLANEOUS

C.A.U.S.E. Game
This game was developed by J.S. Hughes and is designed to be used with the children of alcoholics.
Available from:
 National Council on Alcoholism
 Central Mississippi Area, Inc.
 1510 North State Street
 Jackson, MS 39202

Children of Alcoholics
An information resource directory for publications, audio-visuals, and organizations dealing with children of alcoholic parents is presented.
Available from:
 National Clearinghouse for Alcohol Information
 P.O. Box 2345
 Rockville, MD 20852
 Single copy free of charge. Request MS321.

Children of Alcoholics Screening Test: Test Manual.
30 pages plus order forms, price list, research survey and notebook.
Available from:
 Camelot Unlimited
 17 North State Street
 Suite 1222 — Dept. 18
 Chicago, IL 60602

Family Arena
(15 minutes) 1977
This cartoon filmstrip parodies the family conflicts caused by

alcoholism or other chemical dependency in a family member. It also shows that in a chemically dependent family, denial is the chief symptom and family roles are interrelated. Offers a quiz to see if chemical dependency exists in a family and identifies sources for help.
Available from:
> RMI Media Productions
> 120 West 72nd Street
> Kansas City, MO 64114

Help For Children of Alcoholic Parents
> "You Finish It" Feeling Cards
> Defense Shields
> Defense Masks
> Feeling Charade Cards
> Liquor / Pill Bottle Replicas
> Slogan Stickers
> Handful of Compliments Sheets
> Decision-Making Posters
> Family Mobile with 6 Behavior Cards
> Balloons
> Graduation Certificates
> Carry-All Box
> Training Manual
> Cassette and Film
> Complete 12 piece Kit

Available from:
> Children Are People, Inc.
> 4993 Selby Avenue
> St. Paul, MN 55102
> (612)227-4031

Human Resource Bank, David R. Reese
Compilation which includes development of children of alcoholics education program, child abuse, and families with alcoholics.
Available from:
> David R. Reese

1503 Third Street North
Nampa, ID 83651
(208)467-4431

Newsletters specific to Children of Alcoholics:
ALATEEN TALK
    Published by Al-Anon Family Groups, Inc.
P.O. Box 182
Madison Square Station
New York, NY 10159

COA Review
Thomas W. Perrin, Inc.
P.O. Box 190
Rutherford, NJ 07070

COA
N.Y. Coalition for the COA
P.O. Box 9
Hempstead, NY 11440

CHANGES for and about Children of Alcoholics
US Journal of Drug and Alcohol Dependence
1721 Blount Road
Pompano Beach, FL 33069

FOCUS on Chemically Dependent Families
US Journal of Drug and Alcohol Dependence
1721 Blount Road
Pompano Beach, FL 33069

The NACoA Network
National Association for Children of Alcoholics
31706 Coast Highway, Suite 201
South Laguna, CA 92677

Right From the Start
(9 minutes) 1980
Aimed at pregnant social drinkers, this public education slide-tape presentation discusses a healthy pregnancy from a new

born infant's point of view. Nutrition and exercise are stressed, and the harmful effects of alcohol are explained.
Available from:
> Media Services
> Child Development and Mental Health Center
> University of Washington
> Seattle, WA 98795

The Stamp Game: A Game of Feelings
This game was developed by Claudia Black and the purpose of the Stamp Game is to help players to better identify, clarify and express their feelings.
Available from:
> M.A.C.
> 1850 High Street
> Denver, CO 80218

AGENCIES

Addiction Research Foundation
33 Russell Street
Toronto, Ontario
Canada M55 2S1

Adult Children of Alcoholics
6381 Hollywood Blvd., Suite #685
Hollywood, CA 90028

Al-Anon/Alateen Family Group Headquarters, Inc.
P.O. Box 862
Midtown Station
New York, NY 10018-0862
212-302-7240

Alcoholics Anonymous (AA)
P.O. Box 459
Grand Central Station
New York, NY 10163-1100
212-686-1100

American Humane Association
Children's Division
P.O. Box 1266
Denver, CO 80201
303-695-0811

Child Care Information Center
532 Settlers Landing Road
P.O. Box 548
Hampton, VA 23669
804-722-4495

Child Welfare League of America, Inc.
67 Irving Place
New York, NY 10003
212-254-7410

Children Are People, Inc.
493 Selby Avenue
St. Paul, MN 55102
612-227-4031

Children of Alcoholics Foundation, Inc.
200 Park Ave., 31st floor
New York NY 10166
212-949-1404

Children of Alcoholics:
The New Jersey Task Force
P.O. Box 190
Rutherford, New Jersey 07070
201-460-7912

COA Review
The Newsletter About Children of Alcoholics
P.O. Box 190
Rutherford, NJ 07070

Community Intervention, Inc.
220 South Tenth Street
Minneapolis, MN 55403
612-332-6537

Emotions Anonymous
P.O. Box 4245
St. Paul, MN. 55104

Families Anonymous
P.O. Box 344
Torrance, CA. 90501

National Association for Children of Alcoholics
13706 Coast Highway
Suite 201
South Laguna, CA 92677
714-499-3889

National Clearinghouse for Alcohol Information
P.O. Box 2345
Rockville, MD 20850
301-468-2600

National Council on Alcoholism
12 West 21st Street, 7th floor
New York, NY 10010
212-206-6770

National Institute on Alcohol Abuse and Alcoholism
5600 Fishers Lane
Rockville, MD 20857
301-443-2403

Other Victims of Alcoholism, Inc.
P.O. Box 921
Radio City Station
New York, NY 10019
(212) 247-8087

Parental Stress Service, Inc.
154 Santa Clara Avenue
Oakland, CA 95610
415-841-1750

Parents Anonymous
National Office
22330 Hawthorne
Torrance, CA 90505

Rutgers Center of Alcohol Studies
P.O. Box 969
Piscataway, NJ 08854
201-932-2190

Survivors Network
18653 Ventura Boulevard, #143
Tarzana, CA. 91356